Gelassenheit

Day-by-Day with Meister Eckhart

PHILIP KRILL

authorHOUSE®

AuthorHouse™
1663 Liberty Drive
Bloomington, IN 47403
www.authorhouse.com
Phone: 833-262-8899

Published by AuthorHouse 08/16/2021

ISBN: 978-1-6655-3505-2 (sc)
ISBN: 978-1-6655-3504-5 (e)

Library of Congress Control Number: 2021916610

Print information available on the last page.

'*I pray to God to rid me of God.*'

Meister Eckhart

To

Carrie Lee Hershberger

&

Pat Timon

'We were lost but now we are found'

Lk. 15:24

Introduction

Gelassenheit is a German word with many meanings: relinquishment, surrender, abandonment, submission, detachment, letting go, allowing, acquiescence, etc. Meister Eckhart's favorite term for *Gelassenheit* is *releasement*. Eckhart, like mystics of every age, experienced God as a Mystery of *Releasement. Gelassenheit* involves the whole Trinitarian Life. The Father '*lets go of*' Himself in the begetting of His Son, the Son '*allows*' Himself to be begotten in an intra-Trinitarian act of *Gelassenheit,* and together, Father and Son '*release*' the Holy Spirit, for the salvation of the world.

These meditations on *Gelassenheit* are offered to help us experience God as a Mystery of Divine Releasement. Since the spiritual life is also a progressive growth in interior *Gelassenheit,* the author also hopes that this book will inspire a Trinitarian vision of deification and contemplative prayer.

Meister Eckhart (1260-1328) was a German theologian, philosopher, and mystic. A Dominican priest, his writings, comprised mostly of sermons, were considered heretical during his lifetime but are now considered the mystical gold standard of the Middle Ages.

July 16, 2021
Feast of St. Mary Magdalene

Day 1

Love shines even as my thoughts about You fade, O God, for You are always present to me beyond what I think or feel or do. When I turn to You and accept You in this simple way, I have You in every way and in all things, and You shine out in me as the love that cannot cease.

MEDITATION

The reality of 'God' is prior to our willing and acting. Our ideas about 'God' dissolve before the Presence of God.

PRAYER

Show Yourself, not as another object in a world of objects, but as the Source of all things, O God. Help us discern Your Presence in all that exists.

Day 2

You are the One who is in-yet-beyond the many. You are the Light burning in darkness and the Darkness shining beyond light. You are the Good beyond all that is evil, and the Nothing radiant in all things. You are the nameless One in all we name and the origin that gathers in the end and is active in every beginning. You are the One in my many, the Light in my darkness, the Dark in my light, the Good in my evil and the Nothing in my all. You are the Nameless in my name and the Beginning in my end.

MEDITATION

God is both the center and circumference of our lives. God cannot be located in the cosmos, yet He is the One in whom *'all things hold together'* (cf. Col. 1:17).

PRAYER

We praise You as a Mystery of creative Presence, O God. *'In You we live and move and have our being'* (Acts 17:28).

Day 3

If you want to discover the truth about God, don't strive for things that lie beyond you. Draw your thoughts inward to the Center and seek to become one and simple in your soul. Let go of all that distracts you, all you desire, and come home to yourself, and when you do, you'll become the truth you first sought.

MEDITATION

God is present as the incomprehensible Source of all that exists. God is not another object in a world of objects, but the transcendent Origin of all that is.

PRAYER

Help us discern Your Presence as the mystical Epicenter (*Le Point Vierge*) of reality, O God. Grant us knowledge of You as the ineffable No-thing-ness from which everything comes.

Day 4

You are unending life and love without beginning, and this is the light that You pour into my soul which spills over to all that I am and was and will be. You are love unending and life without beginning, love that becomes nothing but radiance within me.

MEDITATION

God is in the world, and the world is in God, yet God is not the world and the world is not God. The cosmos is permeated by God's Presence, saturated with divine Light, obscured only by human ego.

PRAYER

Expand our vision beyond the world of things, O God. Help us discern the radiance of Your Presence in all creation.

Day 5

If you think you can bargain with God, offering your good works and best intentions in the hope of some reward, think again. Try this instead: desire nothing and become like the unbounded Nothing, which is neither here nor there. Only then, in the Now of this Nothing, will you find only God who wants your works of love as an act of praise, and not your bargaining for some reward beyond this great Nothing.

MEDITATION

In ourselves we are nothing, since all Being comes from God. We have nothing to offer to God other than what God has given us.

PRAYER

Strip us of ego, O Lord, so that in our personal nothingness, we can radiate Your Presence.

Day 6

If someone tells you that God is here or there, pay them no heed. If they tell you that God is this or that, ignore them. For you will only find God when you remove every something and seek him in nothing. You will only see him when you become blind and remove every something from him. If you do this, you will finally have only God, and God will have only you. This is what matters. The rest will take care of itself.

MEDITATION

Relinquishment (*Gelassenheit*) is the way to Presence. God is known only in a *Cloud of Unknowing*.[1]

PRAYER

We do not pray to an unknown God, but to You who are known in Unknowing, O God. Deliver us from our attempts to grasp You with our minds. Help us experience You only in Presence.

---

[1] *The Cloud of Unknowing* is an anonymous work of Christian mysticism written in the latter half of the 14th century. The text is a spiritual guide on contemplative prayer that suggests that the way to know God is to abandon consideration of God's particular activities and attributes, and be courageous enough to surrender one's mind and ego to the realm of 'unknowing', at which point one may begin to glimpse the nature of God.

Day 7

There is in me a radiance that never ceases, and if I had eyes to see into the darkest depths of my heart I would know that this inner spark is all You ever see of me, whether by day or by night. This alone is my one, and Your, only delight.

MEDITATION

Each of us is created perfectly by God. We experience this perfection whenever we enter Presence.

PRAYER

We are '*beautiful in Your sight,*' O God (cf. Song 7:6). Help us to realize our inner beauty by entering Your Presence.

Day 8

If I wish to write on a white tablet, whatever else is written on the tablet, however noble its purport, is a hindrance to me. If I am to write, I must wipe the tablet clean of everything. The tablet is most suitable for my purpose when it is blank. Similarly, if God is to write on my heart, everything else must come out of it until it is really sanctified.

MEDITATION

'God' is the Emptiness from which all things come. To experience God's Presence, we must live with an abiding sense of our no-thing-ness.

PRAYER

Help us encounter You in the Emptiness of Presence, O God. Make our hearts blank pages upon which You can write our true names and reveal our true faces (cf. Rev. 2:17).

Day 9

Some say God is gentle and kind, but I say we only truly know this in the abyss of the godhead where we taste the abundance of God in the darkness before the first day and in the image of his why-less love. So take leave of God for God's sake, and dare to dwell in that single oneness beyond every hope of gain, where nothing separates you from God.

MEDITATION

Seek God beyond all your ideas about God. Rest in God's Embrace by practicing Presence.

PRAYER

Only in the Space of dis-possession (*Gelassenheit*) is Your Presence discovered, O God. Deliver us from words into the wordless world of Your Peace.

Day 10

So you want to find God? Give up thinking you know where to look, or how to think about God. For if you imagine tasting God in only one way, you'll remain small in your thinking and cold in your living. But if you want to find God in the right way, expect to find him in everything in your life - in difficulties and in comforts, in tears and in joy. For if you seek God only in one thing, you'll find him in no thing, for God is in all that is.

MEDITATION

Everything in the world is a Sacrament of God's love, if we have the eyes to discern it. We see the Presence of God everywhere or we see it nowhere.

PRAYER

We must *'become as little children'* (cf. Mt. 18:3) to experience Your Presence, O God. Create in us the childlike openness that allow us to recognize Your Presence everywhere in our lives.

Day 11

How are we born in God? This is a mystery beyond all that we can know, but what we can know is that God is born in us whenever we begin to live without a why.

MEDITATION

God can be known only when we abandon our ideas about God. God is not an object, but the Power of Presence in which objects appear and dissolve.

PRAYER

Bring us into the Space of Presence, O God. Reveal Yourself as the Mystery of Presence that makes our perceptions possible.

Day 12

In God there is nothing but God, and when you come to know all creatures in this nothing, you come to know the nothing that is God. So try to know creatures in the nothing beyond every something, and there find this nothing in every something, which is God. You will either understand this or you will not.

MEDITATION

Because all things find their origin in God, no thing can exist on its own. Yet, God Himself is No-thing. Thus, creation is No-thing from No-thing.

PRAYER

In our contemplation of Your No-thing-ness, O God, help us experience Your Presence. Though nothing in ourselves, we receive ourselves as Presence.

Day 13

One person said they had God, while another lamented God's absence. I say this: we must abandon the God we have in our thinking and believing for God's sake, so that we might come to know God as God truly is - beyond knowing, in a single oneness and pure union.

MEDITATION

One must become an 'a-theist' in order to know God. God is not an object of our knowledge but the ineffable Presence that makes all knowledge possible.

PRAYER

Deliver us from created notions of 'God,' O God. Reveal Yourself to us as the Mystery of Presence in which all things appear.

Day 14

If I knew myself as intimately as I ought, I should have perfect knowledge of all creatures.

MEDITATION

To love is to know, and to know is to understand. *'Perfect love drives out all fear'* (1 Jn. 4:18), and fearless love forgives all things.

PRAYER

Grant us hearts of gold, O God. In Presence, let us know You as the Love in whom all things are to be loved (cf. 1 Jn. 4:8, 16).

Day 15

When you retreat from what is outside of you, you'll taste what true freedom means. Not that you will have no more troubles, but all this will no longer bother you. What to do? Find the inner eye and learn to see your life entirely with it. The rest will follow.

MEDITATION

In Presence we receive the Wisdom to know what to do in any situation. Outside of Presence, we are like wind-chimes banging in the breeze.

PRAYER

Draw us to the Place within where Your Presence dwells, O God. Show us that in the Space of Presence, Your Wisdom is given.

Day 16

A wise teacher once said that what we love we become in love, so when we say that we love God, do we mean that we become God? At first blush, this sounds outrageous, and it is, but it's no less true for all that, for in the love we give - to God or to others - there are not two but one, and in love you are more God than you are yourself, for what you love you become in love. So love - and let the rest be.

MEDITATION

'Those who abide in love abide in God and God in them' (1 Jn. 4:16). When we love, we transcend ourselves and enter the Presence of God.

PRAYER

Fill us with Your Love, O God! Make us instruments of Your Indwelling Presence and Peace.

Day 17

An imaginary God will please and delight you, will satisfy and entice you, but when your thoughts pass away, this imaginary God also disappears. What you need is the essential God within you, not the imaginary one on your lips.

MEDITATION

Thoughts of God are so many wisps of air, evaporating in the caverns of our brains. True apprehension of God occurs in Presence.

PRAYER

Take us beyond our thoughts into the Mystery of Presence, O God. Let us abide with You there in every act of Awareness.

Day 18

If you are one of those who expect to see God with your own two eyes remember: God is not a cow. There is no milk and cheese for you here. When you make of God an object, wanting something, anything, God is not there.

MEDITATION

God is No-where and No-thing. We search in vain for God in the world of objects.

PRAYER

Reveal Yourself as the Source of Presence, O God. Show us that You are the Mystery that makes Awareness possible.

Day 19

Never has a person longed after anything so intensely as God longs to bring a person to the point of knowing him. God is always ready, but we are very unready. God is near to us, but we are very far from him. God is within us, but we are outside. God is at home in us, but we are abroad.

MEDITATION

C.S. Lewis once said that the person in search of God is like the mouse in search of the cat. Enough said!

PRAYER

Awaken us to Your Presence, O God. Show us that in our every breath, our every prayer, Your Spirit is breathing within us.

Day 20

God is not what you think, or even what you believe, because God is a word unspoken, a thought unthought, a belief unbelieved. So if you wish to know this God, practice wonder, do what is good, and cultivate Silence. The rest will follow.

MEDITATION

In silence, God speaks. God is beyond anything we can think about God. God is experienced in Presence or nowhere at all.

PRAYER

In stillness we intuit Your Presence, O God. Keep us peacefully rooted in a sense of Your Indwelling Presence.

Day 21

Nothing can divide you from the way you and God are together. You must remember: You are one in the One in whom there is only one.

MEDITATION

Nothing can separate us from the Presence of God. We are distinct from God, yes, but never separated from Him.

PRAYER

Help us realize our fundamental union with You, O God. Show us our oneness with You in the Mystery of Presence.

Day 22

Know this truth: God is in you like a little castle that rests in your soul, greater than all you can imagine. This castle, which is God, is so simple and one that in it your very soul is one with God and you yourself are finally nothing but God.

MEDITATION

If 'God' is the Source of reality, then nothing is 'real' apart from God. Recognizing our nothingness apart from God is the first step to realize that God and we are one (cf. Jn. 15:5).

PRAYER

You are present within the depths of our being, O God. Help us to see that '*in You we live and move and have our being*' (cf. Acts 17:28).

Day 23

What is our secret entry into Your heart? We find it on the path of letting go of what we thought we knew, arriving at the place where we know nothing of knowing, beyond every notion of love, entering the dark only to find ourselves there, ever one with You.

MEDITATION

God is discovered in every act of surrender (*Gelassenheit*). Letting go of inner possessiveness gains us immediate entry into the kingdom of God.

PRAYER

Grant us a spirit of *Gelassenheit*, O God. Show us that in letting go of all, we receive everything in return (cf. Lk. 18:29-30).

Day 24

At the heart of things is an eternal present moment. When we let ourselves come into an awareness of this Now, we come to know ourselves as a becoming-new without renewal. This is the truth beyond all our worries and needs and hopes, this one eternal present moment.

MEDITATION

The present continually renews itself and everything within it. Experiencing life fully in the present moment is the meaning of eternal life.

PRAYER

Help us experience the redeeming power of the present moment, O God. Reveal the power of the Now as a fountain of living water within us (cf. Song 4:15; Jn. 4:10; 7:38).

Day 25

When I learn to love You simply because You are love, I come to accept myself simply because You made me in love and You never stop making me. When I hold onto this and let go of every doubt, I find Your love in everything and I become love in You and You become love in me.

MEDITATION

Love permeates us completely when we learn to prize *being* over doing. The miracle of existence comes from, and returns to, divine Love.

PRAYER

Grant us the joy of being, O God. Help us to apprehend the act of being as the wellspring of Your creative love.

Day 26

Often I think I should find You within myself, but it isn't so: only when I let go of myself with all my wants and needs, for the sake of Your love, do I find You, for in Your love You go completely outside Yourself to find me.

MEDITATION

With God, there is no inside or outside. All is in God, and God is in all, yet neither is identical with the other.

PRAYER

Show us what total divestment (*Gelassenheit*) means, O God. Help us surrender all to You so we may receive everything from You.

Day 27

I don't like the dark. I'd rather be clothed than naked. Yet You tell me I must let go of all that clothes me - my joys and fears, my worries and even my imaginings - and give myself to the dark emptiness where You wait to be born in me.

MEDITATION

There is no room for God when we are full of ourselves. Only the empty chalice can be filled with the wine of His Spirit.

PRAYER

Grant us the inner stillness that can receive Your Word, O God (cf. Wis. 18:15). Bring us into the dark and silent night of faith where You reveal Yourself to us.

When I seek what You alone can give, what I find is my seeking, like the wager of a business deal in which I hope for payment for my efforts. But You who are always already within me do not seek me, so You do not desire my finding but rather the emptiness by which I might unclutter my life of all that I am, even my faith, even my desire to seek You. This You cannot resist.

MEDITATION

God does not honor our seeking, but our willingness to be found. Our quest for God is actually God's search for us.

PRAYER

Help us realize that in seeking You, we are largely seeking ourselves, O God. Deliver us from narcissistic spirituality and grant us a life of childlike trust (cf. Mt. 18:3).

Day 29

We think of things as this or that, as better or worse, as good or bad, but in God everything is what it is and lives in the perfection of its being. Which is to say that the little fly as it exists in God is nobler than the highest angel is in itself. What then of me? What then of you?

MEDITATION

Rocks and stars, trees and flowers glorify God simply by being what they are. What makes it so difficult for us to follow their good example?

PRAYER

Grant us the simplicity of plants and animals, O God. Help us to learn from these 'guardians of being'[2] how to glorify You by simply being ourselves.

---

[2] See Eckhart Tolle's book, *Guardians of Being: Spiritual Teachings from Our Dogs and Cats.*

Day 30

What You are able to do in me depends on the quality of my life and whether there is enough space for You to act as You wish to do. For my work is simply to shake myself loose of what I think or expect You desire so that You might find in my naked nothingness enough room for You to be the love You ever are and long to set free in me.

MEDITATION

Cultivating inner spaciousness is the key in spiritual living. It is in inner emptiness (*Gelassenheit*) that God works miracles in us.

PRAYER

Help us give You room to operate within us, O God. Evacuate us of ego, so Your Spirit can transfigure our lives.

Day 31

Don't try to find God. Simplify your scattered life, and become one in yourself, then God will find you. The rest will follow.

MEDITATION

Letting ourselves be loved by God is the way to find God. Nothing redounds to our spiritual benefit that is not initiated and brought to completion by God (cf. Phil. 2:13).

PRAYER

Inspire us simplicity of spirit (*Gelassenheit*), O God. Strip from us everything that prevents Your possession of our lives.

Day 32

There is only ever one path you are on when you are on the path to God. Many ways may suggest themselves; many good alternatives may come. Just gather them to that one path that is already yours that is God's that is yours.

MEDITATION

As the saying goes: 'Wherever you go, there you are.' There is no other path to God than the one we are traveling. Do the best you can and leave the rest to God.

PRAYER

Reveal the futility of seeking You in any other way than You are leading us, O God. Deliver us from the spiritual cul-de-sac of comparing ourselves to others.

Day 33

What it is that hurts baffles or befalls me might just be concealing the God whom I love.

MEDITATION

'All things work together for good in the lives of those who seek God' (cf. Rom. 8:28). Saints see every setback as an opportunity to trust God more.

PRAYER

Banish our analysis of what happens to us, O God. Help us to see every obstacle in life as an opportunity to surrender ourselves more completely to You.

Day 34

It's true: sometimes you have to break things if you want to grasp God in them. In the breaking, we allow what's holy to take form in us.

MEDITATION

Nothing happens if nothing happens. One thing we can count on with God: He never allows us to rest content with the *status quo.*

PRAYER

Show us that holiness means being cracked open before You, O God. '*A humble, contrite heart You will not spurn*' (cf. Ps. 51:17), but a haughty, egoistic spirit You reject (cf. Prv. 21:24; Lk. 1:51).

Day 35

To you who know God as God knows you, happiness is heavenly, and, like all blessed ones, you will see only One.

MEDITATION

Seeing God in all things is one thing, but seeing all things in God is quite another. The latter is the real meaning of having a pure heart (cf. Mt. 5:8).

PRAYER

Help us know ourselves as You know us, O God. Beholding our own original perfection in You, we will see only Your goodness in others.

Day 36

The soul that wants nothing but God must forsake everything, even God.

MEDITATION

Since God is no 'thing,' we can never objectify God. We must transcend our ideas about God if we wish to experience the Presence of God.

PRAYER

Our language about You is meaningless unless we recognize its inherent insufficiency, O God. Show us that contemplative prayer joins us to You more surely than spiritual speculation.

Day 37

As long as we have and know who God is, we don't. We are far away. So can you let your notions die? This is the smallest death a soul can undergo before it becomes divine.

MEDITATION

If we can describe it, it is not God. 'Knowledge of God,' cognitively defined, is oxymoronic.

PRAYER

You reveal Yourself to us as the Great *I AM*, O God (cf. Ex. 3:14). Annihilate our ideas of You so we can experience the immediacy of Your Presence (cf. 1 Cor. 2:10).

Day 38

If you want to be ready for and worthy of the Spirit of God, just look inside and see your spiritual being. Can you see how you already resemble what you seek?

MEDITATION

We are made in the '*image and likeness*' of God (Gen. 1:27). As such we are both perfect and nothing. That is, we reflect perfectly the One of whom we are an image, yet as God's image, we possess no being in ourselves other than His reflection.

PRAYER

Help us to appreciate both our beauty and our poverty in You, O God. Show us that we are perfect in every way, so long as we remember that '*You alone are good*' (cf. Mk. 10:18).

Day 39

What I want is joy. What You teach me is that suffering is the way, letting go is the truth, and nothingness is the life. Which is after all what I need.

MEDITATION

Once we realize our nothingness in God, everything else is a breeze. Possessing nothing in ourselves, we have everything if we remain in God (cf. Jn. 15:4-9).

PRAYER

Loosen our death grip on life, O God. Remind us we cannot receive You if we cling to our meager possessions (cf. Lk. 9:24; 17:33).

Day 40

There is a language so beautiful that it is never spoken. There is a deep sort of silence that may never adequately fall into words. That, I tell you, is more valuable than any jewel or any diamond.

MEDITATION

Silence and stillness speak their own language. They communicate that which cannot be said about God without reducing God to a god.

PRAYER

Yours is the Name *'above every other name,'* O God (cf. Eph. 1:21). Reveal Your Presence in the wordless grammar of silence.

Day 41

What You want of me, God, is that I clean the slate, emptying it of all this to make room for the freedom of nothingness where alone You, my God, have room to grow.

MEDITATION

We are '*God's garden*' (cf. 1 Cor 3:9). The more we get rid of the rocks, stones, and weeds of the ego, the more room there is for God to plant His Word in our souls.

PRAYER

Make us fertile seed beds of Your fructifying Presence, O God. Cleanse us of our attachments so Your Spirit may grow within us.

Day 42

I often wonder if I am lovable and love cautiously because I know how easily I can be hurt and my heart broken, but You do not hesitate toward me, since You are all love and only love. When You love, You love without measure, and when You love me in this way, I find who I am and who You are, which is all and ever only love.

MEDITATION

We throw caution to the breeze when love comes our way. Freedom arises when we know God's love.

PRAYER

Envelop us in Your endless Love, O God. Enfold us in Your divine Embrace and tell us our true names (cf. Rev. 2:17).

Day 43

Too often I decide what my life should be and whether there is room in it for You while You sit in a deeper place within me, wondering what it will take for me to make more of all the things in my life - the good and the bad - and so learn to break through to find You in all that is and let You take form in me in all that I was and am and will be.

MEDITATION

In the deepest center of our souls, God waits for us to discover His Presence. Once that happens, present, past, and future are divinized with His Love.

PRAYER

Remind us that while we cogitate about our lives, You are waiting for us to surrender to You, O God. Give us the peace that comes from entrusting all that we were, are, and ever will be to Your care.

Day 44

You are love in everything that is, and it belongs to the perfection of Your greatness that not even my nothingness is far from You.

MEDITATION

We are nothing from Nothing. Since God is No-thing, our existence is a participation in His infinitely perfect No-thing-ness.

PRAYER

All that we are and all that we have come to us as a gift from You, O God. Just as Your goodness is beyond our comprehension, so too is our own.

Day 45

You meet me in my imperfection and You act on me not from the distance of my failings but from the presence of Your perfection which is the way love is.

MEDITATION

God does not see our failures. He sees only His perfect image and likeness within us. One glance from God in our direction and our sins are forgiven.

PRAYER

Sins cannot separate us from You, O God. On the contrary, You use the suffering that comes from our missteps to draw us back to Yourself.

Day 46

When I open my heart to receive You in times of peace and quiet, this is as it should be, but if I close my heart to You when I have lost my way and my life is a mess, and I have failed to know the truth. These differ only for me but not for You, for Your heart opens to me with a single undivided love.

Meditation

The locked doors of our hearts are no obstacle to God's invading Presence (cf. Jn. 20:26). Our obstreperousness is God's opportunity to manifest His indiscriminate Love (cf. Mt. 5:45).

Prayer

When our lives are a mess, awaken us to Your summons to return to You, O God. Make our trust in You as single and undivided as Your love for us.

Day 47

Oh, teach me in each moment of every Now to know that You are the Here in all my wandering and the Yes in all my wondering and the Love in nothing less than everything.

MEDITATION

Everything occurs in the present moment. We will never be closer to God that we are now, because it is never not Now.

PRAYER

Every event is a locus of Your Love, O God. Show us Your Love as the *Power of the Now.*[3]

---

[3] A phrase borrowed from Eckhart Tolle, *The Power of Now.*

Day 48

There is within me a citadel where I am one with You, a place so strong and pure that no one - not even You - dares to look inside, unless You strip Yourself of all Your names and natures. This is the point where You are one and simple, for only there, beyond all doing and thinking and feeling, can You know the one I am, and can I know the one You are.

MEDITATION

God is the center and circumference of our lives, both the within and beyond of our created existence. Living from the Still Point of God's Presence within, become *'partakers of His divine nature'* (2 Pt. 1:4).

PRAYER

Take us beyond ourselves so we can live within ourselves, O God. Show us that with You, the way beyond is the way within.

\

We should not thank You because You love us, but thank You that You are so good that You cannot do anything else!

MEDITATION

Freedom means being *unable not to do* what one must do. 'Following one's conscience' is too timid a phrase to describe the force with which the Spirit compels a saint from within.

PRAYER

Show us the inescapable nature of Your love, O God. Show us that there is nowhere we can flee, including hell, that You are not there to save us with Your infinite Mercy (cf. Ps. 139:7).

Day 50

Most days, I am clear about what is right and wrong, good and bad, in and out, but when I have You close to me in my heart I see how You shine in all that is, especially in my often darkened life.

Meditation

The vision of God dissolves our divisions between good and bad, right and wrong. Seeing all bathed in God's Light, it is impossible not to love everything and everyone.

Prayer

Implant a unified vision in our hearts, O God. Inspire us to live always in Your Light and forget about cursing the darkness.

Day 51

If I wish to become one with You and come to know You as You are, I must set aside my words and become a nothingness spacious enough for Your all-ness. In this You transform me wholly into the one Love You ever are.

MEDITATION

Divine Love purifies human love. Opening ourselves to the Presence of God within, we are cleansed of our sins and deified by His Light.

PRAYER

Show us the simplicity of our divinization in You, O God. Inspire us to surrender to Your Embrace so You can do for us what we cannot do for ourselves.

Day 52

If I hope to find You, I need to let go of all I think I need to know, turning from what I desire to become the emptiness You cannot resist.

MEDITATION

Nature may abhor a vacuum, but God is drawn to one. Seeing a soul empty of self and open to Him, God rushes to fill the emptiness with the fulness of His divine Life.

PRAYER

Divinize us in our nothingness, O God. Show us that *kenosis* (*Gelassenheit*) is the way to *theosis* (deification).

Day 53

Outside of space and time there is no work, nothing is wrought. Time stops. Be there and don't look away because in that place your soul and God are one.

MEDITATION

God is found in the 'pause' between thinking and doing. When we 'take a step back,' or 'take a deep breath,' we experience - if only for a brief moment - the peace of God's Presence.

PRAYER

Help us to abide in Your Presence, O God. Draw us to seek the 'gaps' in our thinking where Your Spirit shines through to console us.

Day 54

I sometimes think You are the reverse of gravity, causing everything to rise, from the heavy earth up to the highest skies, but you show me that Yours is the work of coming down, of weighting what is light so that I, like You, might enter into what is least and raise it up to sound love's delight in heaven's proper height.

MEDITATION

God descends so we can ascend. God descends to the furthest depths of our nothingness to draw us up into the plenitude of His Fulness.

PRAYER

Grant us a share in Your plenitude and in Your mission to *'lift up the lowly,'* O God (cf. Job 22:29; Lk. 1:52). Freight us with the same mercy for others You have shown to us.

Day 55

There is a power that emanates from the spirit within each person and remains totally spiritual. In this power God glows and burns without ceasing, in all his riches, in all his sweetness, and in all his delight. Within this power is so great a joy and so great an immeasurable delight, that no one can fully tell nor reveal it. If any human being, even for a single instant, could see the delight and joy in this, all he may have ever suffered or that God may have wished him to suffer would be a trifle, indeed a nothing. Even more, it would be for him entirely a joy and a pleasure.

MEDITATION

Love turns suffering into joy. We joyfully suffer for the sake of the beloved. If God were our only beloved, would not all our suffering be joy?

PRAYER

Your slightest wish is our command, O God. Enflame us with Your Love such that our suffering pales into nothingness.

Day 56

Even in the shadows of my life where I often tremble with shame. You are present there as the light that ever shines without ceasing. When I turn my heart to that darkness I find that You were there, shining, all along.

MEDITATION

God is never not present. We are never not in perfect union with God. 'Sin' is that which simply obscures, but never disrupts, God's ineradicable oneness with us.

PRAYER

Banish the shadows in our lives with Your uncreated Light, O God. Remind us You are the Light *'the darkness can never overcome'* (cf. Jn. 1:5).

Day 57

Are you looking for God using the same eyes you employ to perceive temporal things? That won't work. God is not like colors in the sky. What you see with those old eyes of yours is something else. It is not God.

MEDITATION

God is not an object like the other objects in the world. Nor is God an Object 'outside' the world. The world is in God and God is in the world, but the world is not God and God is not the world.

PRAYER

Reveal Yourself according to the ways of Your Spirit, O God. Help us to stop looking for You in any way other than as Emmanuel, God-with-us.

Day 58

There are millions upon millions of people, but know that when God looks on any one of them, that one alone receives everything necessary from that singular gaze.

MEDITATION

The quality of God's Mercy is not strained. God sees and loves everyone infinitely, yet each person is also the apple of God's eye.

PRAYER

Show us how Your universal love that is uniquely suited, without compromise, to each of us, O God. Show us how every person is the exclusive focus of Your universal love.

Day 59

It is wicked to expect some specific thing from God. If you asked, you received - and received in full, more than you can imagine or know.

MEDITATION

'*Ask and you shall receive, knock and the door will be answered*' (Mt. 7:7). God is never outdone in generosity.

PRAYER

We do not know how we should pray, O God (cf. Rom. 8:26). Expand our desires to match the infinite largesse of Your Divine Mercy.

Day 60

There is a secret hidden in the heart, a treasure as close to us as our breath, a mystery living in the midst of our soul. Finding it is simple, but may be hard, since to do so we must abandon the self we thought we were and seek the gift that is always ours: this inner spark that no darkness can finally extinguish, though it keeps us from knowing it. This gift is always present to us, if only we have eyes to see. And when we do, we will find its radiance in everything, and at all times, this light that blazes on in a darkness that cannot put it out, this secret that finds us when we risk abandoning ourselves to this presence.

MEDITATION

God is discovered as the inextinguishable Light in the virginal point (*Le Point Vierge*)in our souls.[4] This little point of nothingness is the pure glory of God in us, a pure diamond, blazing with the invisible light of heaven.

PRAYER

Help us live from the virginal point in our being, O God. Transfigure us through Your Presence in the deepest center of our souls.

---

[4] See my book, *Le Point Vierge: Meditations on the Mystery of Presence.*

Day 61

Live into mercy, and you will become what you love, for love unites us in our loving, not in our being. So give yourself to love and love yourself in giving. The rest will follow of its own.

MEDITATION

We become one with what we love. Love conforms the lover to the beloved. Loving God above all things, we become one with Him, partakers of His divinity (cf. 2 Pt. 1:4).

PRAYER

'Love God and do what you will,' said St. Augustine, O God.[5] Transfigure us in Your Love so our actions are filled with Your mercy as a by-product of loving You.

---

[5] St. Augustine, *Sermon on 1 John 4:4-12.*

Day 62

The eye that really matters is the inner eye that beholds what is beyond change. When you retreat from what is outside of you, you'll taste what true freedom means. Not that you will have no more troubles, but all this will no longer bother you. Find the inner eye and learn to see your life entirely with it. The rest will follow of its own.

MEDITATION

To apprehend the Presence of God we must learn to see with inner eyes. *'It is only in the heart that one can see rightly, what is essential is invisible to the eye.'*[6]

PRAYER

Grant us mystical vision, O God. Help us see reality as translucent with Your infinite Light and Love.

---

[6] Borrowed from Antoine de Saint-Exupéry, *The Little Prince.*

Day 63

If you want to reach the highest wisdom, refuse everything you know, abandon all you aspire to be, and seek the darkness of the lowest place of all. Become nothing, and there God will pour out the whole of himself, who is All, with all his strength, and you will see in the light you long for.

MEDITATION

It is in complete surrender (*Gelassenheit*) that we experience the Presence of God. Accepting the nothingness of our own being, we come to know God as the Source of all that is good.

PRAYER

Show us that every breath is a gift from You, O God. Show us that in humble acceptance of our nothingness, You fill us with the infinity of Your Goodness.

Day 64

You will not find me in the usual places. Come to the desert if you'd like to see. Look where you might become lost for a while.

MEDITATION

God is beyond all we can think or say of God. Abandoning our pretentions of reaching God with our thoughts or deeds, God comes to us in our surrender (*Gelassenheit*).

PRAYER

You call us into the 'desert' of relinquishment (*Gelassenheit*) to deify us with Your Love, O God. Inspire us to forsake all to enter Your kingdom within (cf. Lk. 17:21).

Day 65

To find God is to go nowhere. Angels suddenly appear in your path; never mind them. To find God is to go where we are alone with the One, enclosed.

MEDITATION

We must close the doors of our senses, and bolt even more firmly the passageways to our minds, to encounter God in the depths of our hearts. Learning to abide with God within is the essence of the spiritual life.

PRAYER

We need go no further than to descend into our hearts to encounter You, O God. Grant us the perseverance to wait upon You there until You make Your indwelling Presence known.

Day 66

When you are really free you will no longer pine away for freedom. You will be present in this moment. You will be happy to follow God alone in the light that shows us where we are.

MEDITATION

The Power of the present moment - of the Now - is infinite. It is the Presence of God in the temporal world.

PRAYER

If we let go of everything and rest in the Presence of the Now, we can know ourselves as one with You, O God. Grant us the grace to experience the life-changing difference between thinking and being present.

Day 67

No matter how deep the darkness within you, there remains a spark there, and this light wants only this: the naked God as God truly is, and not ideas about God, however true this might be. This spark wants the deep ground that is God - the quiet desert, the simple silence. There, in this innermost place beyond knowing and being, there the spark desires what it needs, and finds what it desires.

MEDITATION

The Spark of God's Life - His Presence - cannot be extinguished in the soul, even by sin. For the soul is *in* God, and in God all things are as eternal and immersed in Divine Love as God Himself.

PRAYER

Lead us into that bottomless journey into the depths of our being where we are one with You, O God. Summon us towards the infinite Horizon of Your Presence where hope springs eternal.

Day 68

Whatever it is that lives and breathes, or loves and seeks meaning or love in return, is loving after God, without whom there is no existence at all.

MEDITATION

Atheism is, strictly speaking, an impossibility. For every adamant denial of truth is an implicit affirmation of it. Otherwise, where would the inspiration for the atheist's love for the truth of atheism come from?

PRAYER

Reveal the transcendent nature of our simplest acts, O God. Show us that in our every act of reaching out, whether in thinking or doing, we are reaching for the Absolute Mystery of Love and Truth which is You (cf. 1 Jn 4:8; Jn. 14:6).

Day 69

Empty a cup completely and keep it empty so that not even air can enter inside. If you can, that cup may cease to be a cup at all. So, you might try emptying yourself of cares and things, of all that now fills you, and you, too, might become something new.

MEDITATION

It is our emptiness (*Gelassenheit*) that makes us what we are - vessels of God's divine glory and instruments of His Peace. Only in our nothingness can God fill us with the infinity of His Peace and Love.

PRAYER

Show us that we are created to be '*the praise of Your glory,*' O God (Eph. 1:12-14). Empty us of anything that impedes the radiance of Your Presence within us.

Day 70

If we could ever see, if only for a moment, the delight and joy that are in God, we would gladly embrace the darkness that comes to us, considering it of little worth, even as nothing, so great would be the measure of our joy and pleasure.

MEDITATION

God, and the things of God, are not simply human things writ large. They are *non-aliud:* completely Other.

PRAYER

Remind us that '*Your ways are not our ways*' (cf. Isa. 55:8), and that '*eye has not seen, ear has not heard, nor has it ever entered any human mind*' what You have in store for those who know You (cf. 1 Cor. 2:9), O God. Grant us a share in the delight and joy that render as nothing all that bedevils us.

Day 71

Stay close now, do not go far from here, for God is only as close as a mirror. If it falls, so falls the image that once appeared there.

MEDITATION

We have no existence as anything other than as a mirror image of God's likeness (cf. Gen. 1:27). As God goes, so go we.

PRAYER

Remind us of our nothingness apart from You, O God (cf. Jn. 15:5). Fill our nothingness with the Fulness of Your Presence.

Day 72

In dark times, even in death, we do well to remember that for God nothing is ever lost or gone, not even in death, since God holds everything that is, even death itself, in the eternal Now of abundant love and endless blessing.

MEDITATION

God's Now is the redemption of the world. In God, all things '*have their being*' and '*all things hold together*' (cf. Col. 1:16-17). Nothing exists or is sustained in being apart from God (cf. Jn. 1:3).

PRAYER

Increase our appreciation for our coinherence with You, O God. Show us that we exist only because we partake of Your pre-eternal Life (cf. Eph. 1:4; Jn. 17:24).

Day 73

Some imagine there is no light in their life but only a long darkness. I say that the light is never absent, always seeking to flow forth within the ground of the soul, but we block it in our confusion and fail to see how it ever shines and burns in us. So if you want to know the light, you must first face the darkness that is in you. Only then will this light overflow your soul and dance with radiance in your life.

MEDITATION

As soon as we face our inner darkness, the Light of God's Peace arises in our hearts. Self-honesty brings the Bliss of self-transcendence.

PRAYER

Show us that Presence - to ourselves and others - brings us Your Peace, O God. Reveal the Presence of Your Light in our experience of self-transcendence.

Day 74

Some truths are as remarkable as they are simple, and this is one such truth: God's nature is to give and give and give, without measure, and God does this at all times - but especially when we are down and out, lost and lonely. God asks only that we take what comes in this gift, which is nothing less than God's very self. When we refuse to do this, we deny who we are and, finally, kill God. So open yourself to this gift and ready yourself for this truth and so learn to become God's joy.

MEDITATION

We are created to the praise of God's glory and recipients of God's own joy (cf. Eph. 1:12-14; Jn. 17:13). We can only do this if we believe, and abide in, the infinity of God's Love.

PRAYER

The abundance of Your Love is inconceivable to us, O God (cf. 1 Cor. 2:9). Awaken us to the infinity of this Love so we can become partakers of Your divine Bliss (cf. Jn. 15:11).

Day 75

If you seek God with prior expectations, you might get what you expect, but you'll know nothing of God - because God always hides in the dark of our knowing. But if you seek God without any idea about who or what God is, you'll find yourself one with the One, and in this light find yourself joined to the One who is always Love, without beginning or end.

MEDITATION

We meet God in the realm of No Mind. God reveals Himself to those who have not made up their minds about Him in advance.

PRAYER

Give us the openness (*Gelassenheit*) of little children, O God (cf. Mt. 18:3). Help us to receive You with innocent anticipation, not with burdensome expectations.

Day 76

Among the miracles ever happening among us, the greatest is this: that God is ever glowing and burning with all his riches, in all that is, even in every darkness we face and in all that we must suffer and endure. God does this constantly and without ceasing, opening to us in just this way a measure of his sweetness and the abundance of his good pleasure.

MEDITATION

Every event, even (especially?) suffering, is an invitation from God to enter into His joy through acceptance and self-awareness. In all things, God works to awaken us to His Presence.

PRAYER

Help us discern Your Presence in everything we encounter, O God. Show us that You slip into our dreary lives with Your transfiguring Love the moment we open ourselves to You.

Day 77

If you were so holy you would not need God at all and your work would leave you calm and confident. If you were so holy you would be imperturbable when others try turning you away from God's presence.

MEDITATION

Nothing can disturb the person continuously aware of God's Presence. Such awareness comes from living fully in the Now.

PRAYER

Show us the difference between analysis and awareness, O God. Show us that practicing Presence is the path to imperturbability and peace.

Day 78

Who can understand this: that God is creating the world not out there, but in the innermost part of the soul, where there is no time nor the light of any image?

MEDITATION

Creation neither began nor ended with the Big Bang. Creation is a continuous outpouring of Divine Love since '*before the foundation of the world*' (cf. Eph. 1:4; 1 Pt. 1:20).

PRAYER

You '*make all things new*,' O God (cf. Rev. 21:5). In You, everything is always '*a new creation*' (cf. 2 Cor. 5:17).

Day 79

Listen closely to the instruction I am going to give you. I could have so vast an intelligence that all the images that all human beings have ever received and those that are in God himself were comprehended by my intellect; however, if I were in no way attached to them, if I did not cling to them, but if I kept myself unceasingly free and void for the beloved will of God and its fulfillment, then I should indeed be a 'virgin,' without the ties of all the images, as truly as I was when I was not yet.

Meditation

Virginity of spirit means being uncluttered by ideas about God. The Presence of God is apprehended only by the virginal heart.

Prayer

Make us spiritual virgins, O God. Purify our inner being so we can receive You unencumbered by theories that obscure Your immediate Presence.

Day 80

Imagine this amazing truth: God is always creating within you, in the heart's darkness, amid the shards of your life and even in the chaos. Even there, God is and you are in the perpetual Now that is Love, in and through you.

MEDITATION

God is the Power in the perpetual Now. God's Presence and God's love permeate everything at every moment in a creative, redemptive manner.

PRAYER

Make us aware of Your constantly creative Love, O God. Reveal our capacity for presence to be Your Presence at work within us.

Here is a truth that we can scarcely imagine: where God is, there is the soul, and where the soul is, there is God. Think about it. When you do, you'll stop looking for God here or there, now or then, and pay attention to where you are and who you are in your soul. Only then will you finally see that the soul and God are one. The rest will be easy.

MEDITATION

Wherever we go, there we are, and so is God. There is no 'outside of God.' Everywhere we go, we land in the same place - God's Embrace.

PRAYER

Direct our gaze inward, not outward, in our search for You, O God. Remind us continuously that You are *'closer to us that we are to ourselves.'*[7]

---

[7] A phrase made famous by St. Augustine (*Confessions* III, 6, 11): *'interior intimo meo et superior summo meo'* ('higher than my highest and more inward than my innermost self').

Day 82

Test for Divine Knowledge: Look at a stick standing in water. It appears bent when it really is straight. For me, it is enough that what I know of God is true in me and is true in God.

MEDITATION

Cognitive knowledge of God is always something of a distortion, like the appearance of a stick in water. God is always greater than that of which we can conceive.

PRAYER

Straighten out our relationship with You by moving us from our heads to our hearts, O God. Show us You cannot be grasped in books but only in the bottomless depths of our being.

Day 83

So you're still longing for God? Your desire won't help you come a single step closer. Give up your desire, which won't help you - and dare to give up God. Then learn to make space in your mind for the nothing God is and find that everything you need lies in this nothingness. This is wisdom truer and stronger than desire.

MEDITATION

God is no 'thing' and can only be contemplated as no-thing-ness. Emptying ourselves of our desire for God and our ideas about God, we discover God in the emptiness.

PRAYER

Lead us to seek You in the realm of 'no mind,' O God. Take us beyond our preconceptions of You to discover You in the nothingness of Your Presence.

Day 84

No one can stop you, hinder, or disturb you, if you are fixed on God alone. For God is always at work inside of you, and what you do and say will be godly, so look out.

MEDITATION

The more we are knowingly one with God, the more our words and actions resonate with divine gravitas. Union with God is the way to peace and spiritual power.

PRAYER

Take possession of our lives such that our words are Your words, our deeds, Your deeds, O God (cf. Gal. 2:20; Mt. 10:20). Anchor us in Your Presence so we radiate Your Love to others.

Day 85

I intensely hope that my book will make the sparks of divine fire buried in you burst out of the earth.

MEDITATION

In the virginal depths of every human heart burns the Presence of the One who created us. This fire of Divine Love is there to consume us, and, through us, to transfigure the world (cf. Ex. 3:2; Lk. 12:49).

PRAYER

Enflame our hearts with the Presence of Your Love, O God. Make us incandescent instruments of Your transfiguring Peace.

Day 86

The most important hour is always the present. The most significant person is precisely the one sitting across from you right now. The most necessary work is always love.

MEDITATION

It is always in the present moment that we discover the Presence of God. Indeed, the kingdom of God *is* the mystery of Presence.

PRAYER

Enlighten us with the Power of the Now, O God.[8] Awaken us to Your Presence in every present moment.

---

[8] See above, n. 3.

Day 87

If the only prayer you ever say in your entire life is thank you, it will be enough.

MEDITATION

Gratitude is our portal into the kingdom of God. In heartfelt thankfulness we enter the space inhabited by God's Spirit.

PRAYER

Give us joyful, grateful hearts, O God. Show us there is no such a thing as a sad saint.

Day 88

What good is it to me that Mary gave birth to the son of God fourteen hundred years ago, if I do not also give birth to the Son of God in my time and in my culture? We are all meant to be mothers of God. God is always needing to be born.

MEDITATION

God comes to birth in those who conceive of Him in love. We all become mothers of God when we experience God's pre-eternal love for us as Father.

PRAYER

Be born anew in us, even as we are reborn in You, O God (cf. Jn. 3:3). Show us that our deification in You and Your glorification in us comprise a single mystery (cf. Jn. 17:22-24).

Day 89

The only thing that burns in hell is the part of you that won't let go of your life: your memories, your attachments. They burn them all away, but they're not punishing you, they're freeing your soul.

MEDITATION

Our attachments are kindling wood for God's purgatorial fires of love. God prunes our dead branches to make us flourish on His Vine (cf. Jn. 15:1-5).

PRAYER

Free us from our attachments so You can be our everything, O God. Annihilate our possessiveness in the purifying Fire of Your Divine Mercy.

Day 90

Above all else, know this: Be prepared at all times for the gifts of God and be ready always for new ones. For God is a thousand times more ready to give than we are to receive.

MEDITATION

We ask for a cupful and God wants to give us the ocean. It's not that our requests of God are wrong, they're too small.

PRAYER

Expand our willingness to receive You, O God. Remind us that *'no eye has seen, nor ear heard, nor the heart of man conceived, what You have prepared for those who love You,'* (1 Cor. 2:9).

Day 91

There is a huge silence inside each of us that beckons us into itself, and the recovery of our own silence can begin to teach us the language of heaven.

MEDITATION

'*The kingdom of God is within*' (cf. Lk. 17:21). Entering inner stillness, we encounter the Presence of God.

PRAYER

Reveal Yourself in inner stillness, O God. Show us the things of heaven in the silence of our hearts.

Day 92

For the person who has learned to let go and let be, nothing can ever get in the way again.

MEDITATION

When all is surrendered, interference with our plans becomes impossible. We discover that the interruptions in our lives *are* our lives, and that our expectations only generate premeditated resentments.

PRAYER

Free us from fear, doubt, and insecurity, O God. Help us to let go and let be, so that Your Peace will replace our worries.

Day 93

Be willing to be a beginner every single morning.

MEDITATION

We are always on the first day of the rest of our lives. It is never not Now, so it is best to practice Presence if we wish to avoid living lives of quiet desperation.

PRAYER

Grant us the gift of always being beginners, O God. Make us childlike in our trust of You, so that the mysteries of Your Presence may continually delight us.

Day 94

The most powerful prayer, one well-nigh omnipotent, and the worthiest work of all is the outcome of a quiet mind. The quieter it is the more powerful, the worthier, the deeper, the more telling and more perfect the prayer is. To the quiet mind all things are possible. What is a quiet mind? A quiet mind is one which nothing weighs on, nothing worries, which, free from ties and from all self-seeking, is wholly merged into the will of God and dead to its own.

MEDITATION

God reveals Himself in the realm of *Mushin* (No Mind).[9] A quiet mind - empty of thought yet suffused with alert attentiveness - is where God's Presence is known.

PRAYER

Bring us to that state of inner stillness where the uncreated Light of Your Presence illumines us, O God. Divinize us in our interior, silent surrender (*Gelassenheit*) to You.

---

[9] **Mushin** in Japanese and **Wuxin** in Chinese is a Zen expression meaning being free from mind-attachment.

Day 95

What we plant in the soil of contemplation, we shall reap in the harvest of action.

Meditation

Contemplation is openness to the infinite. When we look upon the world with contemplative vision, the whole world appears *'charged with the grandeur of God.'*[10]

Prayer

Give us a certain kind of beatific vision even in this world, O God. Let us see all things as bathed in the Light of Your infinite Love.

---

[10] From the first line of Gerard Manley Hopkins' poem, *God's Grandeur.*

Day 96

Stillness is where creativity and solutions are found, and it is in the darkness that one finds the light.

MEDITATION

Creativity emerges from a place beyond analytic thinking. It is when we let go of our preconceptions (*Gelassenheit*) that the genuinely new can reveal itself.

PRAYER

Show us that death and resurrection are the fundamental template for the whole of creation, O God. Show us that nothing dies that is not reconfigured and restored with a new creativity that bespeaks Your Wisdom.

Day 97

Apprehend God in all things, for God is in all things. Every single creature is full of God and is a book about God. Every creature is a word of God.

Meditation

Being participates in the Source of Being, i.e., 'God.' God is in the world and the world is in God, but God is not the world, and the world is not God.

Prayer

Help us appreciate our coinherence with You, O God. Show us that *'apart from You we can do nothing'* (cf. Jn. 15:5), but rooted in You *'all things are possible'* for us (cf. Phil. 4:13).

Day 98

Between God and me there is no 'Between'.

MEDITATION

We are in God, and God is in us, but we are not God, and God is not us. God is the *Source* of our existence, at once beyond and within the creatures He has made.

PRAYER

You are *'closer to us that we are to ourselves,'* O God.[11] Help us appreciate both Your immanent and transcendent Presence.

---

[11] See above, n. 6.

Day 99

The eye through which I see God is the same eye through which God sees me. My eye and God's eye are one eye, one seeing, one knowing, one love.

MEDITATION

'*Even before a word is on my lips,*' God is aware of it (cf. Ps. 139:4) God is the Soul of our souls, the Heart of our hearts.

PRAYER

Your envelop us in the infinite Embrace of Your divine Love, O God. Show us that any love we may exhibit for You is itself a result of Your pre-eternal love for us.

Day 100

Spirituality is not to be learned by flight from the world, or by running away from things, or by turning solitary and going apart from the world. Rather, we must learn an inner solitude wherever or with whomsoever we may be. We must learn to penetrate things and find God there.

MEDITATION

There is no need to flee to a monastery to discover God present in all things. 'To see the world in a grain of sand' is all we need to do.[12]

PRAYER

Help us discern Your Presence in all that is, O God. In Presence, let us behold the perfection of all You have made.

---

[12] 'To see a World in a Grain of Sand, And a Heaven in a Wild Flower, Hold Infinity in the palm of your hand…' are the opening lines of William Blake's poem, Auguries of Heaven.

Theologians may quarrel, but the mystics of the world speak the same language.

MEDITATION

Abiding in Presence, we acquire mystical vision. Mystical vision is seeing all things as God intends them, not as we would have them.

PRAYER

Grant us a share in Your creative vision, O God. Help us perceive the deep-down beauty of all You have made.

Day 102

To be full of things is to be empty of God. To be empty of things is to be full of God.

MEDITATION

Like negative space in a work of art, our emptiness (*Gelassenheit*) before God allows Him to illumine us with His Presence. It is the background of God's Love, not the foreground of our existence, that glorifies God.

PRAYER

Awaken us to our nothingness before You, O God. Show us that it is our self-emptying (*Gelassenheit*) that Your Presence in us is unveiled.

Day 103

Wisdom consists in doing the next think you have to do, doing it with your whole heart, and finding delight in doing it.

MEDITATION

A Zen-like mindfulness can teach us a lot about how to walk humbly in the Presence of God. Unselfconsciousness is the key to allowing God to have His way with us.

PRAYER

'*Lead, kindly Light!*'[13] Show us the way into Your Presence one step at a time. Give us the Wisdom to do the next thing pleasing to You.

---

[13] See the poem by John Henry Newman with the same title.

Day 104

God is not found in the soul by adding anything but by a process of subtraction.

MEDITATION

The kingdom of God does not admit storm troopers. Surrender and letting go (*Gelassenheit*) are the keys to God's kingdom.

PRAYER

Grant us the docility needed for union with You, O God. Show us that it is in surrendered hearts (*Gelassenheit*) that You take up Your abode (cf. Jn. 14:23; Rev. 3:20).

Day 105

Treat all things as if they were loaned to you without ownership - whether body or soul, sense or strength, external goods or honors, house or hall - everything.

MEDITATION

All we possess is on loan from God. We are given what we have so God may be glorified in us.

PRAYER

What do we have that we have not received from You, O God (cf. 1 Cor. 4:7)? Let gratitude be our gift to You.

Day 106

To the extent that you eliminate ego from your activities, God comes into them - but no more and no less. Begin with that, and let it cost you your uttermost. In this way, and no other, is true peace to be found.

MEDITATION

Light and darkness cannot co-exist. God's Presence dispels the darkness, God's Spirit evicts the ego.

PRAYER

Divest us of our possessiveness so we can be filled with Your Spirit, O God. Dissolve the egoic obstacles to our deification.

Day 107

As God can only be seen by His own light, so He can only be loved by His own love.

MEDITATION

God is at work in us, '*both to will and to work for His own good pleasure*' (Phil. 2:13). God's desire is to transform us into '*the praise of His glory*' (cf. Eph. 1:12-14).

PRAYER

Awaken us to our beloved nothingness in You, O God. We are '*a hole in a flute that the Christ's breath moves through - listen to the music.*'[14]

---

[14] Hafiz, *The Christ's Breath.*

Day 108

Nobody at any time is cut off from God.

MEDITATION

It is impossible ever not to be in union with God. Perfect union with God - our deification - comes about when we give ourselves unreservedly to God's Embrace.

PRAYER

Move us from our '*natural union*' with You to a '*transformative union*' with You, O God.[15] Anchor us so deeply within Yourself that it is '*no longer we who live but You who live in us*' (cf. Jn. 15:5; Gal.2:20).

---

[15] The distinction between a 'natural' or substantial' union with God and a 'transformative' union of 'likeness' with Him is that St. John of the Cross. See *Ascent to Mt. Carmel*, II, 5. 3.

Day 109

To the quiet mind all things are possible.

MEDITATION

In stillness, God's speaks. Supernatural wisdom is communicated in silence to those who enter the prayer of the heart.

PRAYER

You communicate the *'peace that passes all understanding'* to those who quiet their minds, O God (cf. Phil. 4:7; Mt. 6:7). In the stillness of contemplative prayer, manifest Your Presence to us.

Day 110

You need seek God neither below or above. He is no farther away than the door of the heart.

MEDITATION

God is the 'within' of every 'without.' God inhabits the *inscape* of the world, always *'closer to us that we are to ourselves.'*[16]

PRAYER

We seek You in vain when we seek You outside ourselves, O God. For You, 'above' is 'within,' and 'beyond' is 'beneath.'

---

[16] See above, n. 7. *Inscaping* the heart is a recurring theme in the poetry of Gerard Manley Hopkins.

Day 111

The soul is created in a place between Time and Eternity: with its highest powers it touches Eternity, with its lower Time.

MEDITATION

We live in two worlds - the kingdom of God and the *civitas* of time and space. If we give our hearts to heaven, our lives on earth will be happy (cf. Lk. 18:29-30).

PRAYER

You have created us to be *'gods in God,'* O God (cf. Jn. 10:34-35).[17] Help us to love You *'above all things'* and, as a by-product, *'love our neighbor as ourselves'* (cf. Lk. 10:27).

---

[17] A recurring phrase in the early church to describe our deification (*theosis*) in Christ. As St. John of Damascus says, speaking for the patristic tradition, we 'become by *adoption* what Christ is himself by *nature.'* See his *On the Orthodox Faith* 4.13.

The more deeply we are our true selves, the less self is in us.

MEDITATION

Our true self lies buried beneath the many layers of ego, ever-perfect in the God who created us. Sin can never disfigure the perfect '*image and likeness*' of Himself that God created us to be (cf. Gen. 1:26-27).

PRAYER

Strip us of ego so that our true self can fill the whole of us, O God. As Your *image* becomes more fully Your *likeness* within us, our ego is banished forever.

Day 113

The very best and noblest attainment in this life is to be silent and let God work and speak within. Therefore it is said: 'In the midst of silence the secret word was spoken to me'.

MEDITATION

Silence invites surrender, and surrender leads to silence. In silent surrender, God speaks within us with wisdom *'too deep for words'* (cf. Rom. 8:26).

PRAYER

Reveal Your secret wisdom in the silence of our hearts, O God. Illumine us from within with Your uncreated Light.

Day 114

People should not worry as much about what they do but rather about what they are. If they and their ways are good, then their deeds are radiant. We should not think that holiness is based on what we do but rather on what we are, for it is not our works which sanctify us but we who sanctify our works.

MEDITATION

Good and evil reside in the human heart (cf. Mt. 15:18). Our actions are good insofar as they flow from a heart devoid of ego and united to God's Spirit.

PRAYER

Purify our hearts of their impurities, O God. Work within us both the desires and the actions pleasing to You (cf. Phil. 2:13).

Day 115

Truly, it is in darkness that one finds the light, so when we are in sorrow, then this light is nearest of all to us.

MEDITATION

Sorrow serves as the catalyst for deeper surrender (*Gelassenheit*) to God. Concealed in every moment of darkness is the silent voice of God urging us to seek the Light.

PRAYER

Help us discern Your Presence in the negative spaces in our lives, O God. Remind us nothing happens that You are not there with Your divine Love (cf. Rom. 8:35-39; Ps. 139:7-12).

Day 116

Love is the root of all joy and sorrow. The price of inaction is far greater than the cost of making a mistake.

MEDITATION

As the cliché goes - it is better to have loved and lost than not to have loved at all. God writes straight with crooked lines, but He cannot re-write our lives at all if we don't mark up the paper.

PRAYER

Free us from remaining stuck in our fears, doubts, and insecurities, O God. Lead us kindly, but insistently, from ego into Spirit.

Day 117

The very best and highest attainment in this life is to remain still and let God act and speak in you.

MEDITATION

Surrender to God is not quietism. Openness to God is alert attentiveness, unspoiled by any mental agenda.

PRAYER

Grant us the courage and patience to wait on You, O God. Teach us prayer of the heart where, in silent stillness, Your Word enters and inspires us.

Day 118

God expects but one thing of you, and that is that you should come out of yourself in so far as you are a created being and let God be God in you.

MEDITATION

Our capacity for self-transcendence is God's Presence within us. When we take a step back, or take a time out, we give God room to be Himself in us.

PRAYER

Help us move out of our own way so You may have Your way with us, O God. Show us that it is in the gaps and pauses of our lives that You work best.

Day 119

The seed of God is in us: Pear seeds grow into pear trees, hazel seeds into hazel trees ... And God seeds into God.

MEDITATION

We are made fruitful by the Life of God within us. He is *'the Vine and we are the branches,'* a participatory relationship that glorifies God and divinizes us (cf. Jn. 15:1-5).

PRAYER

Reveal our destiny as deification in You, O God. Show us we are created to be, through Your Life in us, *'gods in God.'*[18]

---

[18] See above, n. 17.

Day 120

If you love yourself, you love everybody else as you do yourself. As long as you love another person less than you love yourself, you will not really succeed in loving yourself but if you love all alike, including yourself, you will love them as one person and that person is both God and man.

MEDITATION

Humanity is as a single Person to God (cf. Gal. 3:28; Col. 1:71; Eph. 2:21). What God desires for one, He desires for all, i.e., divinization in His pre-eternal Love (cf. Jn. 17:21-24).

PRAYER

Help us see our oneness in You, O God. Show us that You are one with us, and we are one with You and each other.

Day 121

He who would be serene and pure needs but one thing, detachment.

MEDITATION

God's most inward nature is *kenosis*, self-emptying (*Gelassenheit*). As God's '*image and likeness*' (Gen. 1:26), we too are most ourselves when divesting ourselves of self.

PRAYER

Grant us a share of Your inner detachment (*kenosis, Gelassenheit*), O God. Show us that in letting go, we are filled with Your self-divesting Love.

Day 122

There exists only the present instant. There is no yesterday nor any tomorrow, but only Now.

MEDITATION

God is pure Actuality. Thus, everything that comes from God - i.e., all creation - always occurs in the present moment.

PRAYER

Awaken us to the deep-down freshness in things, O God.[19]

---

[19] As Hopkins says, '*There lives the dearest freshness deep down things.*' See above, n. 10.

Day 123

Jesus went into the temple and boldly drove out those that bought and sold. When all was cleared, there was nobody left but Jesus. Observe this, for it is the same with us: when he is alone he is able to speak in the temple of the soul. If anyone else is speaking in the temple of your soul, Jesus will keep still, as if he were not at home. He is not at home wherever there are strange guests-guests with whom the soul holds conversation, guests who are seeking to bargain. If Jesus is to speak and be heard, the soul must be alone and quiet.

MEDITATION

God doesn't speak until we stop talking. God requires our undivided attention if we are hear to the *'small, still voice'* of God's Spirit (cf. 2 Kg. 19:12).

PRAYER

Teach us how to pray contemplatively, O God. Rid our monkey-minds of their clamor and open us to the whisperings of Your Spirit.

Day 124

If we seek God for our own good and profit, we are not seeking God.

Meditation

To love God above all things means letting go of bargaining with God. We must replace a *transactional* relationship with God for one of profound *intimacy*.

Prayer

You fulfill us in Your Love when we let go of our purchase on You, O God. Show us that in letting go (*Gelassenheit*) we discover who You truly are.

Day 125

God is like a person who clears his throat while hiding and so gives himself away. God lies in wait for us with nothing so much as love.

MEDITATION

God wants to be found by us. He gives us signals of His Presence but never compels us to seek Him.

PRAYER

Work in us both the desire to find You, O God, and the fulfillment of this desire. Become our everything such that we leave all else behind to pursue You.

Day 126

That which a man acquires by contemplation he should spend in love.

MEDITATION

Like a beautiful lake that has both inflow and outflow, we must give to others what we have received. Is there anything we have not received? Is there anything we can withhold from God or from others?

PRAYER

Fill us so completely with Your Light and Love that we naturally give light and warmth to others, O God. Fill us with Your Life in contemplation so we can share Your Life in action.

Day 127

You will have peace to the extent that you have God, and the further you are away from God the less you will be at peace. Thus you may measure your progress with God by measuring your peace or the lack of it.

MEDITATION

Serenity is the measure of our connection with God. *'If we can keep our heads when all about us are losing theirs and blaming it on us; if we can trust in God when others doubt us and make allowances for their doubting too'* - then we can be confident our union with God is deepening.[20]

PRAYER

Be our unshakeable Rock, O God. Let the strength of Your Love banish our fears and fill us with Your Peace (cf. 1 Jn. 4:18; Jn. 14:27).

---

[20] Borrowed from the opening lines of Rudyard Kipling's poem, *'If'*: *'If you can keep your head when all about you are losing theirs and blaming it on you; If you can trust yourself when all men doubt you, but make allowance for their doubting too...then you'll be a man, my son.'*

Day 128

Our bodily food is changed into us, but our spiritual food changes us into it.

MEDITATION

Life in God is one of ascension through descent. Descending into our nothingness, we are assimilated into the Life of God.

PRAYER

When touched by Your Spirit, we are changed into Spirit-bearers, O God. Abiding in Your Presence, we become *'partakers of Your divinity'* (cf. 2 Pt. 1:4).

Day 129

Existence itself stands in need of nothing, for it lacks nothing, whereas everything else needs it, because outside of it there is nothing. Nothingness stands in need of existence, as a sick man lacks health and is in need. Health has no need of a sick man. To want nothing, therefore, characterizes the highest perfection, is fullest and purest existence.

MEDITATION

In God, absence is fulness and plenitude is emptiness. God is the Divine No-thing-ness from which all things spring..

PRAYER

The world is Your gift to Yourself, O God. Though in need of nothing, You create everything that is so that it may share in Your Divine No-thing-ness.

Day 130

The eye with which I see God is the same eye with which God sees me.

MEDITATION

Just as our eyes cannot see themselves, God cannot be 'seen' as an object of our perception. God can be only known intuitively as the Source of our capacity to perceive.

PRAYER

Reveal Yourself as the Source of our seeing, O God. Show Yourself as the *'Light in which we see light'* (cf. Ps. 36:9).

Day 131

In the nakedness of his essence which is above every name, God penetrates and falls into the naked essence of the mind which is itself without proper name. This is the castle into which God enters, in his being rather than in his acting, giving to the mind the divine and deiform being.

MEDITATION

When we think '*with the mind of God*,' our lives become as peaceful as God's. God is God by nature, we are 'gods' by participation in the mind of God, given us by God's Spirit (cf. 1 Cor. 2:16; Phil. 2:5).

PRAYER

Assimilate our thoughts to Yours, O God. Conform us to Yourself such that we look upon the world as You do.

What does God do all day long? He gives birth. From the beginning of eternity, God lies on a maternity bed giving birth to all. God is creating this whole universe full and entire in this present moment.

MEDITATION

Creation is not a single Big Bang, but a continuous 'calling into being' of that which was not before God summoned it into existence. Creation is always in the present moment, not the distant past.

PRAYER

Awaken us to the miracle that every creature has its being only as a participation in You, O God. Show us that, like a song, all that exists does so only so long as You continue to sing.

Day 133

God cannot know himself without me.

MEDITATION

We have been known by God since '*before the foundation of the world*' (Eph. 1:4). This implies, in some sense, that God has never known Himself without knowing, and loving, us as well.

PRAYER

Help us bask in Your pre-eternal knowledge of us, O God. Enflame our hearts with assurances of Your everlasting union with us.

Day 134

God is at home; it's we who have gone out for a walk.

MEDITATION

As the saying goes: if God seems far away, who moved? It is impossible not to be in union with God, yet God seems distant from us when we neglect His Presence.

PRAYER

Awaken us to Your indwelling Presence, O God. Remind us there is nowhere we can go, nor anything we can do, that can separate us from Your Love (cf. Rom. 8:38-39; Ps. 139:7).

Day 135

Everything is meant to be lost, that the soul may stand in unhampered nothingness.

MEDITATION

Life is designed by God - believe it or not - so things will go wrong. This is because our problems are God's opportunities to inspire greater reliance on Him (cf. Jn. 9:3; Rom. 11:32).

PRAYER

'*All things work for good in the lives of those*' who trust in You, O God (cf. Rom. 8:28). Ensure us that every obstacle we encounter can lead us into deeper surrender to You.

Day 136

The outward man is the swinging door; the inner man is the still hinge.

MEDITATION

Everything in our lives revolves around a 'virginal point' in the depths of our being where we and God are one. There, God speaks to us in silent stillness.

PRAYER

Teach us the prayer of the heart, O God. Attune our inner ear to the silent music and quiet whispers of Your Spirit (cf. Rom. 8:26; 2 Kg. 19:12).

Day 137

People should not worry so much about what they do but rather about what they are.

MEDITATION

Being precedes doing. It is out of the heart, not vice versa, that all our actions, good or evil, come (cf. Mt. 15:18).

PRAYER

Purify us from within, O God. If You divinize us at our roots, all our actions will give You glory.

Day 138

Whether you like it or not, whether you know it or not, secretly all nature seeks God and works toward God.

MEDITATION

Everything created finds its origin and fulfillment outside itself. Like flowers opening to the sun, the cosmos itself expands in search of the God who makes it.

PRAYER

Show us that our limitations are Your invitation to find fulfillment in You, O God. Show us that the desire for goodness and truth are hardwired into us so we transcend ourselves and discover what we are searching for in You.

Day 139

The shell must be cracked apart if what is in it is to come out, for if you want the kernel, you must break the shell. Therefore if you want to discover nature's nakedness, you must destroy its symbols, and the farther you get in, the nearer you come to its essence. When you come to the One that gathers all things up into itself, there you must stay.

MEDITATION

Peeling an onion only brings us smelly hands. Peeling away our layers of ego, however, we discover *'the pearl of great price'* (cf. Mt. 13:46), i.e., the experience of God's Presence within.

PRAYER

Show us the interiority of all things as the nexus of their participation in You, O God. Help us discern You as the invisible, sustaining Source of all that is.

Day 140

God wants nothing from you but the gift of a peaceful heart.

MEDITATION

God demands nothing of us, since all we have - including our desire for, and achievement of, good words - is a gift from God. Like a good mother, God only wants us to be happy, filled with His peace and bliss.

PRAYER

Fill us with Your peace and bliss, O God. You have made us *'partakers of Your divine nature'* (cf. 2 Pt. 1:4) to share in Your eternal joy (cf. Jn. 15:11).

Day 141

Do not think that saintliness comes from occupation. Rather, it depends on what one is. The kind of work we do does not make us holy, but we may make it holy. However 'sacred' a calling may be, it has no power to sanctify.

MEDITATION

Never confuse your state in life - married, clergy, single - with your vocation. Anyone's vocation is an inner calling, working itself out in a chosen state in life.

PRAYER

Remind us that our true selves are hidden in You, O God (cf. Col. 3:3). Show us that by following the deepest desires of our hearts we can will find vocational fulfillment.

Day 142

When a man sees the one in all things, he is above mere understanding.

MEDITATION

Saints see connections where unconscious persons see only data. Awakening to the Presence of God happens when the connections between all things become clear.

PRAYER

Elevate our spiritual imaginations to perceive Your Presence in all creation, O God. Reveal the world, in its seamless variety, as a kaleidoscopic sacrament of Your Love.

Day 143

Every creature is a word of God.

MEDITATION

God spoke and things came to be (cf. Gen. 1:3). Things are called into being by the creative Word of God.

PRAYER

Every object in the universe is a word in Your infinite lexicon of Love, O God. Help us discern Your Voice in the melody of creation.

Day 144

God is equally near in all creatures.

MEDITATION

God does not need non-discrimination legislation to treat all people fairly. Our equality in dignity springs from our participation in God's own divine Love.

PRAYER

Show us that heaven is not beyond the clouds, but just beyond our insecurities, O God. Show us that every person we meet is a living tabernacle of Your Presence.

Day 145

You may call God love; you may call God goodness. But the best name for God is compassion.

MEDITATION

The compassion of the saints comes from a connection to a Love that is out of this world. Saints love themselves and others as instruments of Divine Love.

PRAYER

'*Even if a mother were to forget her child*' - a human impossibility - You would not forget us, O God (cf. Isa. 49:15). Awaken us to the unfathomable depths of Your divine compassion.

Day 146

God is a great underground river that no one can dam up and no one can stop.

MEDITATION

The life of the world is made possible by the River of Life irrigating the whole of existence (cf. Rev. 22:1-3). The universe continues to expand because God cannot *not* create.

PRAYER

Open our hearts to the effulgence of Your creative love, O God. Keep us from imagining limits to what You can and cannot do.

Day 147

One must not always think so much about what one should do, but rather what one should be. Our works do not ennoble us, but we must ennoble our works.

Meditation

'If the tree is sound, its fruits will be good' (cf. Mt. 12:33). If our hearts are pure, our actions will be filled with light and love.

Prayer

Cleanse us from the inside out, O God (cf. Lk. 11:39). Purify our hearts so we can see You, and others, with a deified vision.

Day 148

Where and when God finds you ready, he must act and overflow into you, just as when the air is clear and pure, the sun must overflow into it and cannot refrain from doing that.

MEDITATION

We are created to be translucent with God's Light and Spirit. God divinizes us with His glory to the extent we are ready to receive it.

PRAYER

Make us ready to become *'partakers of Your divine nature,'* O God (cf. 2 Pt. 1:4). Prepare us to assume our destiny as 'gods in God.'[21]

---

[21] See above, n. 17.

Day 149

The outward work will never be puny if the inward work is great.

MEDITATION

Spiritual power flows from within. Transformative union with God, taking place in the heart, turns us into icons of God's supernatural peace and love.

PRAYER

Accomplish Your desires within us, O God. Divinize us in Your love and make us instruments of Your peace.

Day 150

The most powerful prayer, one well-nigh omnipotent, and the worthiest work of all is the outcome of a quiet mind. The quieter it is the more powerful, the worthier, the deeper, the more telling and more perfect the prayer is.

MEDITATION

One moment of silent Presence is more powerful than a lifetime of good works. Presence manifests the power of God; good works are the happy by-product of a person who knows how to be present.

PRAYER

Show us the power of Presence over projects, O God. Make us persons of Presence who radiate Your peace even when we are doing nothing.

Day 151

Nothing will be able to hinder us, if we desire and seek God alone, and take pleasure in nothing else.

MEDITATION

God is everything for us or God is nothing to us. In the spiritual life, there is no middle ground.

PRAYER

Apart from You, *'we can do nothing,'* O God (cf. Jn. 15:1), but in union with You, *'all things are possible'* for us (cf. Phil. 4:13; Mk. 9:23). Unite us to Yourself so we can say *'it is no longer we who live but You who live in us'* (cf. Gal. 2:20).

A man may go into the field and say his prayer and be aware of God, or he may be in Church and be aware of God; but, if he is more aware of Him because he is in a quiet place, that is his own deficiency and not God's. God is alike present in all things and places and is willing to give Himself everywhere so far as lies in Him.

MEDITATION

We are enjoined to '*pray without ceasing*' (1 Th. 5:17). Creation is God's cathedral where communion with God in prayer can be enjoyed anywhere, anytime.

PRAYER

Dissolve the distinctions we make between 'sacred' and 'secular,' O God. Show us that all things are holy, and that every moment and every place afford us the opportunity to commune with You in prayer.

Day 153

He knows God rightly who knows Him everywhere.

MEDITATION

Love is not geographically restrained. As with any human love, when we love God truly, we love Him everywhere always.

PRAYER

To love You is to be permeated with the Love and Light that You are, O God (cf. 1 Jn. 1:5; 4:8). *'In Your Light we see light'* (cf. Ps. 36:9), and in Your Love, we love You and all You have made.

Day 154

A man should orient his will and all his works to God and, having only God in view, go forward unafraid, not thinking, am I right or am I wrong? One who worked out all the chances before starting his first fight would never fight at all. If, going to someplace, we must think how to set the front foot down, we shall never get there. It is our duty to do the next thing: go straight on, that is the right way.

MEDITATION

Ethical deliberation is for those who have not acquired a connatural knowledge of God. Deification eliminates the need for moral casuistry and makes for saintly *parrhesia*.[22]

PRAYER

Make us unselfconscious in our love for You, O God. Make us so one with You that doing what You desire becomes second nature for us.

---

[22] *Parrhesia* literally means 'to speak everything' and by extension 'to speak freely,' 'to speak boldly,' or, simply, 'boldness.' It is a term applied to many of the saints to describe their scandalous familiarity with which they often speak to God.

Day 155

To seek God by rituals is to get the ritual and lose God in the process.

MEDITATION

Never mistake a symbol for what it signifies. True, some symbols efficaciously communicate a sampling of what they signify, but no set of symbols can substitute for possession of the things to which they point.

PRAYER

You are the Mystery that can never be captured through symbol or ritual, O God. Deepen our appreciation of Your Presence, both within and beyond its sacramental expression.

People who have let go of themselves are so pure that the world cannot harm them.

MEDITATION

True detachment makes us impervious to the opinions of others. An untouchable innocence is given to those who surrender their lives completely to God.

PRAYER

Grant us the interior relinquishment (*Gelassenheit*) that makes us saints, O God. Give us the freedom of spirit that enables us to '*bless our enemies and pray for those who hurt us*' (cf. Lk. 6:28).

Our best chance of finding God is to look in the place where we left him.

MEDITATION

The moment we take control of our lives, the Spirit of God flees from us. The moment we loosen our grip on life, the Spirit alights within us.

PRAYER

Deliver us from our game of hide-and-seek with You, O God. Grant us the spirit of surrender (*Gelassenheit*) to that You can possess us with Your Spirit.

Day 158

The knower and the known are one. Simple people imagine that they should see God as if he stood there and they here. This is not so. God and I, we are one in knowledge.

MEDITATION

We are never not one with God. If God feels distant, it is because we have lost - or not learned - how to cultivate our rootedness in Him.

PRAYER

Make Your Presence palpable to us, O God. In the depths our being, show us that we know You even as You know us (cf. 1 Cor. 13:12).

Day 159

I need to be silent for awhile, worlds are forming in my heart.

MEDITATION

'*Out of the abundance of the heart, the mouth speaks*' (Lk. 6:45). Only words in-breathed by the Spirit of God have the power to inspire.

PRAYER

Fill our words with the breath of Your Spirit, O God. Inspire us to listen to Your Spirit before we speak.

Day 160

Jesus might have said, 'I became man for you; if you do not become God for me, you wrong me.'

MEDITATION

God's desire is that we become *'partakers of His divine nature.'* God became man so we could become God.[23]

PRAYER

Your *kenosis* (self-emptying) is our *theosis* (divinization), O God. Awaken us to our true destiny as 'gods in God.'[24]

---

[23] St. Athanasius, *On the Incarnation*, 54.
[24] See above, n. 17.

Day 161

Behold how all those people are merchants who shun great sins and would like to be good and do good deeds in God's honor, such as fasts, vigils, prayers, and similar good deeds of all kinds. They do all these things so that our Lord may give them something, or so that God may do something dear to them. All these people are merchants.

MEDITATION

A transactional, or commercial, relationship with God is spiritual death (cf. Gal. 3:10). A god who can be bribed or bargained with is not the God who only desires our trustful surrender (*Gelassenheit*).

PRAYER

Save us from trafficking in religious transactions, O God. Grant us the simple, childlike trust that opens the treasures of Your kingdom to us (cf. Gal. 2:16; Rom. 9:32).

Day 162

A life of rest and peace in God is good; a life of pain lived in patience is still better; but to have peace in a life of pain is best of all. Remember this: all suffering comes to an end. Whatever you suffer authentically, God has suffered from it first.

MEDITATION

Pain becomes 'suffering' only when it is accepted and embraced. To 'suffer' means 'to allow.' It is the power of Allowing-ness (*Gelassenheit*) that makes pain redemptive 'suffering.'

PRAYER

Help us 'suffer' life on life's terms, O God. Grant us the kind of acceptance (*Gelassenheit*) that brings *'the peace that passes all understanding'* (cf. Phil. 4:7).

Day 163

God is at his greatest when I am at my least.

MEDITATION

Our weakness is God's opportunity. Vulnerability is the crack in our character where God can infuse His healing balm.

PRAYER

Open us to Your strength in our weakness, O God. Help us see that You work best when we relinquish our bravado.

Day 164

The more we have the less we own.

MEDITATION

With God, poverty is wealth, and self-emptying is self-fulfillment (cf. Phil. 2:6-11). When filled with the Spirit of God, our possessiveness disappears.

PRAYER

Show us that detachment (*Gelassenheit*) is both a result of, and condition for, union with You, O God. Make us ready to receive You by surprising us with Your Presence.

Day 165

When I experience Love I must go to God. When I experience non-attachment God must come to me.

MEDITATION

Nature may abhor a vacuum, but God delights in it. When God sees a soul empty of expectations or possessiveness, He becomes its fulness.

PRAYER

Empty us of all preconceptions of You and others, O God, so we may be filled with Your comfort and peace (cf. Jn. 14:16).

Day 166

Nature's intent is neither food, nor drink, nor clothing, nor comfort, nor anything else in which God is left out. Whether you like it or not, whether you know it or not, nature secretly seeks, hunts, tries to ferret out the track on which God may be found.

MEDITATION

All things come from God, and all things are oriented towards God. Everything is united to God, and in God *'all things hold together'* (cf. Col. 1:17).

PRAYER

Show us that it is the fulfillment of our nature to be divinized in You, O God. Reveal Yourself as the Beginning and End - Alpha and Omega (cf. Rev. 22:13) - of our lives.

Day 167

This is my only and permanent complaint, that vulgar people, empty of the Spirit of God, want to judge solely by their human thinking what they listen to or read in the Bible, which has been pronounced and written by the Holy Spirit and in the Holy Spirit.

MEDITATION

Only the Spirit of God understands '*the deep things of God*' (cf. 1 Cor. 2:10). Scripture offers no inspiration except through the whispers of the Spirit who wrote it.

PRAYER

Deliver us from biblical literalism, O God. Show us that You are the Word within the Word, who's Spirit alone can reveal You to us (cf. Jn. 16:13).

Day 168

God holds each of us by a string. When we sin, we cut the string. But God ties it up again, making a knot. Each time our wrongdoing cuts the string, God ties another knot drawing us up closer to Him.

MEDITATION

We can never cut ourselves off from God. Such theological gibberish knows nothing of God's inescapable love.[25]

PRAYER

Free us from tying ourselves up in knots, worrying about being rejected by You, O God. Reveal Yourself as the God who delivers us from our sins better than Houdini escaping from danger.

---

[25] See Thomas Talbott, *The Inescapable Love of God.*

Day 169

Whatever you say of God is untrue.

MEDITATION

Since God is No-thing, nothing we can ever say about God is adequate to His majesty. God is known in His effects, never as God knows Himself.

PRAYER

Show us that our speculations about You are so many wisps of ignorance, O God. Remind us that the only words really appropriate for You are songs of adoration.

Day 170

God who is without name - he has no name. God is ineffable, and the soul in its ground is likewise ineffable, just as ineffable as God.

MEDITATION

Existence is altogether a divine mystery. All created things are no-thing other than what God knows them to be. We are opaque to ourselves but known perfectly to God.

PRAYER

Curb our hubris whenever we think we know anything of You, ourselves, or others, O God. Remind us our lives are *'hidden in You'* (cf. Col. 3:3) - a mystery as ineffable as You Yourself.

God is intelligence occupied with knowing itself.

Meditation

Artificial intelligence (AI) has nothing on God. Linear learning, no matter how artificially advanced, knows nothing of the Source of living consciousness.

Prayer

Our capacity for awareness and self-transcendence is Your gift to us, O God. The intuition of Your Presence in our acts of knowing brings a divine bliss no machine can produce.

Day 172

To get at the core of God at his greatest, one must first get to the core of himself, for no one can know God who has not first known himself. This core is a simple stillness, which is unmoved itself but by whose immobility all things are moved, and all receive life.

MEDITATION

Every object has an invisible center of gravity from which its coherence derives. In all objects, but especially us, this 'virginal point' of coherence is one with the Presence of God.

PRAYER

At the point of absolute stillness in the center of our being, we receive a generative connection with Your Presence, O God. Help us live from this deepest center of our existence, vibrant and vibrating with Your Life and Light.

Day 173

No one is forgotten. It is a lie, any talk of God that does not comfort you.

MEDITATION

There is nothing outside of God. Wherever we move, wherever we turn, we are immersed in the ocean of God's merciful Presence.

PRAYER

In You *'we live and move and have our being,'* O God (cf. Acts 17:28). Keep us from being like fish who are unable to recognize the water they swim in.

Day 174

In silence man can most readily preserve his integrity.

MEDITATION

We can't go wrong if we curb our tongues when tempted to display our knowledge (cf. Jas. 3:5). Contemplative silence speaks louder than words.

PRAYER

You pray within us *'with sighs too deep for words,'* O God (cf. Rom. 8:26). When we speak, let it be Your Spirit speaking through us.

Day 175

God is nearer to me than I am to myself; He is just as near to wood and stone, but they do not know it.

Meditation

Inanimate objects fulfill God's will simply by being themselves. The same applies to us once we realize it is '*not simply we who live but God who lives within us*' (cf. Gal. 2:20).

Prayer

Increase our awareness of Your indwelling Presence, O God. Awaken us to the mystery of our rootedness in You.

Day 176

We must come into a transformed knowing, an unknowing which comes not from ignorance but from knowledge.

MEDITATION

When we recognize the limits of our own understanding, we mysteriously transcend them. Humbly acknowledging our finitude brings us a taste of God's infinite peace.

PRAYER

Fill us with the bliss that comes from recognizing You as God, O God. The more we come to know ourselves, the more we realize that *'apart from You we are nothing'* (cf. Jn. 15:5).

Do not think that saintliness comes from occupation; it depends rather on what one is. The kind of work we do does not make us holy, but we may make it holy.

MEDITATION

Being precedes doing. If we knew our very existence as the unconditioned gift of God that it is, our actions would be automatically holy.

PRAYER

Any human holiness is a participation in Your sanctity, O God. Remind us we are nothing apart from You, but that in You we receive all things, including whatever holiness we enjoy.

Day 178

God is at home. We are in the far country.

MEDITATION

God is one with us in the depths of our being. Living mostly in our thoughts, we cannot discern the Presence of God within but feel as if God is far away.

PRAYER

Awaken us to Your indwelling Presence, O God. Move us from our heads into the depths of our hearts where You abide.

Day 179

To grasp God in all things - this is the sign of your new birth.

MEDITATION

Shifting from object consciousness into Presence allows us to see all things abiding in God without compromising God's transcendence. The world is in God and God is in the world, but the world is not God and God is not the world.

PRAYER

Grant us a pan-*en*-theistic vision, O God. Help us see all things in You, and You in all things, without conflating or confusing the cosmos with Your transcendent Presence.

Day 180

To be sure, our mental processes often go wrong, so that we imagine God to have gone away. What should be done then? Do exactly what you would do if you felt most secure. Learn to behave thus even in deepest distress and keep yourself that way in any and every estate of life. I can give you no better advice than to find God where you lost him.

MEDITATION

To be aware of our failures is to have already overcome them. To recognize we have lost contact with God is the Spirit of God reawakening us to our connection with God.

PRAYER

Keep us in close connection with You, O God. Re-establish that connection by making us aware when, through too much thinking, we seem to have lost it again.

This much is certain: when a man is happy, happy to the core and root of beatitude, he is no longer conscious of himself or anything else.

MEDITATION

Our experience of joy reveals our self-transcendence. We are created by God to become supernaturally blissful in God's divine Beatitude.

PRAYER

We aspire to a life of deification in You, O God. Grant us a created share in Your infinite Joy.

Day 182

God does not work in all hearts alike, but according to the preparation and sensitivity He finds in each.

MEDITATION

Though a *'jealous lover'* (cf. Deut. 4:24), God is also patient and kind. *'The bruised reed He breaks not, the smoldering wick He does not quench'* (cf. Isa. 42:3; Mt. 12:20). God works with each of us according to our capacity to receive Him.

PRAYER

We glorify You for adapting Your salvific love to the parameters of our neediness, O God. We praise You for Your patience in getting us ready to enter Your kingdom of infinite love.

Day 183

Let God work in you, give the work to God, and have peace. Don't worry if He works through your nature or above your nature, because both are His, nature and grace.

MEDITATION

God's *'ways are not our ways,'* nor ours His (cf. Isa. 55:8). We should give up trying to figure out God and simply let Him have His way with us.

PRAYER

Grant us a true spirit of relinquishment (*Gelassenheit*), O God. Show us that in our absolute surrender to You, You manifest Your Presence to us.

Day 184

I will be silent and will hear what God will say in me. If God wishes to speak to me, let him enter. I will not go out.

MEDITATION

Listening is the key to experiencing the Presence of God. In the silence of the heart, God speaks.

PRAYER

Attune us to the whispers of Your Spirit, O God. Remind us that You pray within us *'with sighs too deep for words'* (Rom. 8:26).

Things are all made from nothing; hence their true source is nothing.

Meditation

We have no 'being' other than that which God give us. All is gift. Knowing our own nothingness is the key to finding happiness in God.

Prayer

In poverty of spirit (*Gelassenheit*), we discover Your Presence, O God. In our nothingness, You reveal the gratuity of Your Love.

Day 186

A free mind is one which is untroubled and unfettered by anything, which has not bound its best part to any particular manner of being or worship and which does not seek its own interest in anything but is always immersed in God's most precious will. There is no work which men and women can perform, however small, which does not draw from this its power and strength.

MEDITATION

Religion is no substitute for a relationship of reliance on God. Spiritual surrender (*Gelassenheit*) is the end and purpose of religious ritual.

PRAYER

One act of letting go (*Gelassenheit*) is more pleasing to You than a mountain of religious piety, O God. Remind us that childlike openness You is '*the one thing necessary*' that '*will not be taken from us*' (cf. Lk. 10:42).

Day 187

It is permissible to take life's blessings with both hands provided you know yourself prepared in the opposite event to take them just as gladly. This applies to food and friends and kindred, to anything God gives and takes away. As long as God is satisfied you can rest content. If he is pleased to want something else of you, still rest content.

MEDITATION

The greatest enjoyment in life comes, not from life's pleasures, but from our willingness to receive everything as God's gift. Our judgments about what's good and what's evil (cf. Gen. 2:17) often prevent such willingness.

PRAYER

Grant us true freedom of spirit, O God. Grant us the kind of detachment (*Gelassenheit*) that is not stoic indifference but blissful surrender to Your superior Wisdom.

God is greater than God.

MEDITATION

If the human spirit is self-transcendent, God is even more so. God is the 'Ever-greater' Mystery of Divine Love who defies description and transcends our cognitive comprehension.

PRAYER

Grant us a mystical appreciation of You as 'Absolute Mystery,' O God.[26] Keep us from trying to domesticate Your transcendental Presence.

---

[26] 'Absolute Mystery' is Karl Rahner's term for pointing to the incomprehensibility of God.

The soul must long for God in order to be set aflame by God's love. If the soul cannot yet feel the longing, then it must long for the longing. To long for the longing is also from God.

MEDITATION

The very desire for God is the action of God within us. Being alert to the whispers of the Spirit is at the heart of the spiritual life.

PRAYER

You are at work within us long before it occurs to us to search for You, O God. Awaken us to the action of Your Spirit within.

Day 190

I tell you the truth, any object you have in your mind, however good, will be a barrier between you and the inmost Truth.

MEDITATION

Thoughts, as important and inevitable as they are, impede our experience of pure Presence. Only a mind devoid of objects can apprehend things of the Spirit.

PRAYER

Awaken us to the difference between thinking and 'being present,' O God. Show us how the Presence transcends yet perfects our thinking.

We are all meant to be mothers of God, for God is always needing to be born.

MEDITATION

God transcends gender, yet our awareness of God must be constantly 'reborn' within us. In this sense, God is need of 'mothering' within us.

PRAYER

Manifest Your Presence in acts of re-birthing within us, O God. Sustain our awareness of Your Presence as appearing ever new, never old.

Day 192

We are celebrating the feast of the Eternal Birth which God the Father has borne and never ceases to bear in all eternity. But if it takes not place in me, what avails it? Everything lies in this, that it should take place in me.

MEDITATION

So long as our experience of God is purely intellectual, we do not really 'know' God. The Presence of God is experienced as always new, always fresh; otherwise, God is not known at all.

PRAYER

Move us from our heads to our hearts so we can experience Your indwelling Presence, O God. Remind us You are always *'closer to us that we are to ourselves.'*[27]

---

[27] See above, n. 7.

Day 193

To be properly expressed, a thing must proceed from within, moved by its form: it must come, not in from without but out from within.

MEDITATION

The ideal *form* of our lives - physically, emotionally, spiritually, vocationally - is known by God since '*before the foundation of the world*' (cf. Eph. 1:12-14). It takes a lifetime (or more) to awaken to this fact.

PRAYER

Grant us an intuitive grasp of our eternal identity in You, O God. Help us align our thoughts and actions with the mystical form of our lives.

For a heart to be perfectly ready it has to be perfectly empty. In this condition it has attained its maximum capacity.

MEDITATION

Poverty is wealth, as far as God is concerned. The only vessels He can fill with His divinizing Presence are those empty of ideas about how God operates.

PRAYER

Relieve us of our theories about You, O God, so we can experience the transcendent immediacy of Your Presence. Show us that our conceptions of You are no substitute for transforming union in You.

Day 195

The soul loves the body, [for] the body is more in the soul than the soul is in the body.

MEDITATION

Who we are expresses itself through our bodies. Our bodies are the sacraments of our souls.

PRAYER

Help us see ourselves, not as *'human beings having a spiritual experience, but as spiritual beings having a human experience,'* O God.[28] Awaken us to the transcendent nature of our embodied existence.

---

[28] A paraphrase of a statement by Pierre Teilhard de Chardin

All God wants of us is a peaceful heart.

MEDITATION

There is no disturbance in the Life of God. As *'partakers of God's divine nature'* (cf. 2 Pt. 1:4), we are created to be vessels and instruments of God's Peace.

PRAYER

Make us instruments of Your Peace, O God. Surfeit our lives with *'the peace that passes all understanding'* (cf. Phil. 4:7).

Day 197

I am what I wanted and I want what I am.

Meditation

In God there is no gap between being and doing. *'God is love'* (1 Jn. 4:8, 16), thus God cannot do anything but love.

Prayer

Grant us contentment with who You have made us to be, O God. Show us that each of us is an inexpressible, unrepeatable icon of Your Divine Love.

Whoever has God truly as a companion, is with him in all places, both on the streets, and among people, as well as in church, or in the desert or in a monastic cell..

MEDITATION

God is everywhere, or God is no where. God is everything to a person, or God is nothing to a person. There is no middle ground.

PRAYER

Grant us a truly 'catholic,' i.e., all-encompassing, love for You, O God. Help us see and love You in all things and see and love all things in You.

Day 199

For persons who possesses God alone, keeping their gaze fixed upon God, all things become God for them. Such people be a God in all their deeds and in all the places they go, and it is God alone who is the author of all their deeds.

MEDITATION

Saints are those whom we recognize as somehow possessed of God. Without necessarily even speaking of God, their words and actions bespeak a Power greater than themselves.

PRAYER

Possess us with Your Spirit of wisdom and love, O God. Help us know intuitively how best to serve You in every situation.

Day 200

God must act and pour himself into you the moment he finds you ready. Don't imagine that God can be compared to an earthly carpenter, who acts or doesn't act, as he wishes; who can will to do something or leave it undone, according to his pleasure. It is not that way with God. Where and when God finds you ready, he must act and overflow into you, just as when the air is clear and pure, the sun must overflow into it and cannot refrain from doing that.

MEDITATION

A divine synergy exists between God's inflow and our readiness to receive Him. The moment He discerns our willingness, He begins our transformation.

PRAYER

You are Gift and Giver, O God. You inspire our desire to seek You and satisfy this desire. Make us worthy of Your deifying love.

Day 201

Whoever possesses God in their being has Him in a divine manner, and He shines out to them in all things. For such persons, all things taste of God and in all things it is God's image that they see.

MEDITATION

Normally, we see the world as *we* are, not as it is. When we are indwelt by God, we see the world as *He* does, not as we do.

PRAYER

Deify our vision, O God. Enable us to see all things as You do, not as we do.

Day 202

What good is it that Christ was born [2,000] years ago if he is not born now in your heart?

MEDITATION

Lacking a sense of the immediacy of God, we turn God into an external object. Contemplative prayer reveals that God is *'closer to us that we are to ourselves.'*[29]

PRAYER

Center us in contemplative prayer so we can know Your immediate Presence, O God. Help us to enter Your divine embrace.

---

[29] See above, n. 7.

Day 203

There is in the soul a something in which God dwells, and there is in the soul a something in which the soul dwells in God.

MEDITATION

At the virginal point in the center of our being, we are one with God and God is one with us. Our true identity is in God (cf. Col. 3:3; Jn. 17:23), yet we are not identical with God.

PRAYER

Awaken us to our coinherence with You, O God. Show us that there is nowhere we can go that we are not held in love by You.

Day 204

Man goes far away or near but God never goes far-off. God is always standing close at hand, and even if he cannot stay within he goes no further than the door.

Meditation

Like a faithful pet but infinitely greater, God cannot be put off, even by our worst behavior. It is not in God's nature to reject anything of what He has made (cf. Jn. 6:37).

Prayer

Even when we are deaf to Your call, You stand '*at the door of our hearts knocking,*' O God (cf. Rev. 3:20). Help us to know You as always close at hand.

He who would be what he ought to be must stop being what he is.

MEDITATION

Relinquishing our ego is a never-ending task. We must continually let go of who we think we are if God is to reveal our true identity in Him (cf. Jer. 1:5; Col. 3:3; Rev. 217).

PRAYER

Save us from ourselves, O God. Keep us from mistaking our ego for our true identity in You.

Day 206

Philosophers say the soul is double-faced, her upper face gazes at God all the time and her lower face looks somewhat down, informing the senses. The upper face, which is the summit of the soul, is in eternity and has nothing to do with time: it knows nothing of time or of body.

MEDITATION

Implicitly, our gaze is always turned towards God, even when we are preoccupied with external tasks. Our souls intuitively know that the goodness and beauty we seek in our daily pursuits are found only in God.

PRAYER

Awaken us to the transcendental yearnings of our souls, O God. Show us that any activity that energizes us is Your Spirit touching our innermost being.

My Lord told me a joke. And seeing Him laugh has done more for me than any scripture I will ever read.

MEDITATION

What would a truly personal relationship with God feel like? Doubtless it would include an exchange of intimacies that would scandalize our religious sensibilities.

PRAYER

In the light of Your smiling Face we cannot keep from singing, O God. Let us enter the joy of Your Presence with the blessed giddiness of little children.

Day 208

There is something in the soul that is so akin to God that it is one with Him. It has nothing in common with anything created.

MEDITATION

We are created beings sustained by the One who is No-thing and No-where. God is present within us without localization.

PRAYER

Awaken us to Your coinherence with us, O God. Help us intuitively grasp Your ineffable, sustaining Presence of Love.

Day 209

When I think of God's Kingdom, I am compelled to be silent because of its immensity, because God's Kingdom is none other than God himself with all His riches.

MEDITATION

'Going to heaven' means being in experiential union with God. Heaven is not beyond the clouds; it's just beyond our fears.

PRAYER

Awaken us to the immediacy of Your Presence, O God. Reveal Yourself as the Power of Now.

Day 210

Only those who have dared to let go can dare to re-enter.

MEDITATION

A popular song intones, '*Freedom's just another word for nothing left to lose.*'[30] Only those who have relinquished everything to God can come and go as they please in their lives in God.

PRAYER

You are a Mystery of Divine Letting Go (*Gelassenheit*), O God. Lavished by Your gratuitous Love, make us instruments of Your divine Releasement.

---

[30] Janis Joplin, *Me & Bobby McGee.*

An image is not of itself; nor is it for itself. It has its origin in that of which it is the image, nor does it owe anything to this. An image receives its being immediately from that of which it is an image. It has one being with it and it is the same being. In exactly the same way you should live: You should be in him and for him, and not in yourself and for yourself.

MEDITATION

We have no more existence in ourselves than an image in a mirror. It is only the One of whom we are the '*image and likeness*' (Gen. 1:26) who truly exists.

PRAYER

Remind us that we are but partakers of Your own Actuality, O God. Only in You do we '*live and move and have our being*' (cf. Acts 17:28).

Some people want to see God with their eyes as they see a cow, and to love Him as they love a cow - for the milk and cheese and profit it brings them. This is how it is with people who love God for the sake of outward wealth or inward comfort. They do not rightly love God, when they love Him for their own advantage.

MEDITATION

God is not an object that can be possessed, or a supernatural figure with whom we can bargain or argue. We exist for the sake of God, not vice versa.

PRAYER

Everything we possess we receive as a gift from You, O God. Deliver us from the temptation to get our greedy hands on You.

Day 213

If you're frightened of dying and you're holding on, you'll see devils tearing your life away. If you've made your peace, then the devils are really angels freeing you from the earth.

MEDITATION

Suffering is parasitic on fear. No fear, no suffering. Pain, yes, suffering, no. This is because love - which is perfect trust - *'casts out all fear'* (1 Jn. 4:18).

PRAYER

Help us die to the fear of death, O God. Show us that in dying before we die, we have *'already passed from death to life'* (cf. Jn. 5:24).

If I say that God is good, that is not true. God is not good. I am good, and if I say that God is wise, that is not true. I am wiser than he is.

MEDITATION

Nothing said of us can be said of God in the same way it can be said of us. Any excellence that pertains to us exists in God only analogically and always in a pre-eminent way.

PRAYER

'*Your thoughts are not our thoughts, O God, nor are Your ways our ways. As the heavens are higher than the earth, so are Your ways higher than ours*' (cf. Isa. 55:8-9). Keep us from speaking about You as if You were only a larger version of ourselves.

Day 216

Nothing in all creation is so like God as stillness.

MEDITATION

God is the incomprehensible Mystery of No-thing-ness in which the universe exists. The ineffable silence of God makes creation possible.

PRAYER

In the stillness of our hearts You reveal Your Presence, O God. Attune us to the sounds of silence in which Your voice can be heard.

Day 217

As long as I am this or that, I am not all things.

MEDITATION

Identification with labels is the action of the ego and the death of the spirit. The golden string of Presence connects all people, while our propensity to categorize each other alienates us.

PRAYER

Save us from the alienation of labeling, O God. Show us that each person is a mystery of Presence, greater than anything we can say of them.

A question arises whether the joys of the angels who guard us are equal to those of the angels in heaven, or whether they are diminished by the fact that they protect and serve us. No, they are certainly not, for the work of the angels is the will of God, and the will of God is the work of the angels. Their service to us does not hinder their joy nor their working. If God told an angel to go to a tree and pluck caterpillars off it, the angel would be quite ready to do so, and it would be his happiness, if it were the will of God.

MEDITATION

There is no gap between the will of God and the obedience of the angels. God's slightest wish is their greatest desire. Would that we were like the angels!

PRAYER

Grant us the holy indifference of the angels, O God. Remind us that You write straight with crooked lines, and that our real joy consists in following Your Spirit.

Day 219

Truth is something so noble that if God could turn aside from it, I could keep the truth and let God go.

MEDITATION

The truth of God is deeper than that of which the human mind can conceive. The splendor of any truth flows from the Splendor of God from whom all truth proceeds.

PRAYER

Attune us to the Truth that passes all understanding, O God. Catch us up in the fulness of Your Truth which is the fulfillment of all our desires.

God has infused sufficiency and pleasure into creatures, but the root of all sufficiency and the essence of all measure God has kept in himself. The sun, although it illumines the air and penetrates it by its light, does not take root there. Thus the brightness of the air ceases when the sun disappears. That is how God communicates himself to his creatures.

MEDITATION

The cosmos participates in God, but God does not participate in the universe. God is the unparticipatible Source of all that is.

PRAYER

You are the Source of all being, O God. Grant us an appreciation of Your unconditioned Presence as the taproot of our existence.

Day 221

Whatever God does, the first outburst is always compassion.

MEDITATION

God cannot *not* love. '*God is love, and all who abide in love abide in God*' (1 Jn. 4:16).

PRAYER

Grant us a share in Your unfailing compassion, O God. Make us as loving in action as You are by nature.

Day 222

In this breaking-through, I receive that God and I are one. Then I am what I was, and then I neither diminish nor increase, for I am then an immovable cause that moves all things.

MEDITATION

We were known by God '*before the foundation of the world*' (Eph, 1:12-14). As such we are one with God from all eternity - God in us, us in God. This is a mystery of asymmetric coinherence that gives us a share in the power and beauty of God Himself.

PRAYER

Help us realize our dignity as Your predestined sons and daughters, O God. Help us break through our spiritual torpor to apprehend our destiny as Your adopted children (cf. Gal. 4:5-6; Jn. 1:12).

Day 223

Once a man came to me that he had given away much landed property and many goods for his own sake so that he might save his soul. Then I thought: 'How little and how insignificant is what you have let go of! It is blindness and foolishness for you to continue looking at all you've let go of. If, however, you've let go of yourself, then you've really let go.'

MEDITATION

It is not our possessions, but our possessiveness, which we need to relinquish. Loosening our death grip on live, we begin to live as God intended.

PRAYER

Dispel our fears of letting go, O God. Show us that what looks like death to the ego is the path to life in the Spirit.

Day 224

Time is what keeps the light from reaching us. There is no greater obstacle to God than time: and not only time but temporalities, not only temporal things but temporal affections; not only temporal affections but the very taint and smell of time.

MEDITATION

In Presence, time stands still, and we receive a taste of divine bliss. When we step out of Presence, analysis takes over and time becomes our enemy.

PRAYER

Deliver us from the suffering that comes from linear thinking, O God. Transport us beyond time into the omnipresent space of Presence.

Day 225

There are plenty to follow our Lord half-way, but not the other half. They will give up possessions, friends and honors, but it touches them too closely to disown themselves.

MEDITATION

It is not enough to get rid of our possessions if we continue to covet them in our hearts. It is our possessiveness, not our possessions, that impede our transformation in God.

PRAYER

Inspire us to follow You in complete relinquishment (*Gelassenheit*), O God. Remind us that only '*those who lose their lives can find them*' (cf. Lk. 17:33).

Day 226

Even now one rarely hears of people achieving great things unless they first stumble in some respect.

Meditation

Suffering is often the pathway to peace. For when we let go of trying to change the things we cannot, the serenity of God is given.

Prayer

God, grant us the serenity to accept the things we cannot change, the courage to change the things we can, and the wisdom to know the difference.[31]

---

[31] The Serenity Prayer.

Day 227

The moral task of man is a process of spiritualization. All creatures are go-betweens: we are placed in time that by diligence in spiritual business we may grow liker and nearer to God. The aim of man is beyond the temporal - in the serene region of the everlasting Present.

MEDITATION

Human life is both a gift and a task. God desires that our '*natural union*' with Him in our creation be perfected in a '*transformative union*' through our practice of Presence.[32]

PRAYER

Transfigure us '*from one degree of glory to another,*' O God (cf. 2 Cor. 3:18). Grant us the grace of total releasement (*Gelassenheit*) that we may glow with Your divine Light.

---

[32] See above, n. 15.

Day 228

Know that when you seek anything of your own, you will never find God, because you do not seek God purely. You are seeking something along with God, and you are acting just as if you were to make a candle out of God in order to look for something with it. Once one finds the things one is looking for, one throws the candle away. This is what you are doing.

Meditation

Belief in God is not an instrument we can use to get what we want in life. A true believer holds a utilitarian approach to God in contempt.

Prayer

Teach us to worship You rightly, O God. Show us that total surrender (*Gelassenheit*) is the form of faith acceptable to You (cf. Ps. 51:16-17).

Day 229

The greatest power available to man is not to use it.

MEDITATION

The relinquishment of power (*Gelassenheit*) is the kind of power exercised by God. God subverts '*the powers and principalities*' in the world by refusing to use their instruments of power (cf. Col. 2:15).

PRAYER

Show us the wisdom of not fighting evil with evil, O God. Remind us what our mothers taught us as children: two wrongs never make a right.

Day 230

When you are thwarted, it is your own attitude that is out of order.

MEDITATION

We are our own greatest enemies. As Chesterton said, in response to the question, *'What's wrong with the world?'*: 'I am.'[33]

PRAYER

Help us to *'judge not lest we be judged'* (cf. Mt. 7:1). Show us that every accusation against another is an indictment of ourselves.

---

[33] G. K. Chesterton, *What's Wrong with the World.*

Day 231

St. Augustine cries, 'Lord I cannot love you, but come in and love yourself in me.' He tells us to discard our own mode of nature, then the divine nature will flow in and be revealed. Also St. Paul says we must put off our own natural form and put on the form of God: 'It is no longer I who live, but Christ who lives in me' (Gal. 2:20).

MEDITATION

Letting go of who we think we are is necessary if God is to reveal His own name for us (cf. Rev. 2:17). Only when we know ourselves as God sees us will we know who we truly are.

PRAYER

Our lives are hidden in You, O God (cf. Col. 3:3). Show us who we are beyond ego and persona.

Day 232

I do not find God outside myself or conceive him except as my own and in me.

MEDITATION

We belong to God, and God belongs to us - not as a possession to keep but as a gift to be shared.

PRAYER

Show us what intimacy with You looks like, O God. Awaken us to our coinherence with You and our inter-connection with all You have made.

Day 233

I have a capacity in my soul for taking in God entirely. I am as sure as I live that nothing is so near to me as God.

MEDITATION

God is *'closer to us than we are to ourselves.'*[34] In God *'we live and move and have our being'* (Acts 17:28). All things find their coherence in Him.

PRAYER

Awaken us to the differentiated unity of Your creation, O God. Show us that, in You, all things are given to us (cf. 1 Cor. 3:21-23).

---

[34] See above, n. 6.

Day 234

No one knows what the soul is. But what we do know is, the soul is where God works compassion.

MEDITATION

Every person has a soft spot in the heart where the Spirit of God abides. God is the Soul of our souls, the Source of our existence at the center of our being.

PRAYER

Draw us into the epicenter of our souls where Your compassion reigns supreme, O God. Bathe us in the transfiguring light of Your Divine Mercy.

What our Lord did was done with the intent, and this alone, that he might be with us and we with him.

MEDITATION

God is always *Emmanuel* - God-with-us. 'With-ness' defines the character of God. We are with God, and God is with us, yet we are not God and God is not us.

PRAYER

We are never without You, O God, and You are never without us (cf. Eph. 1:12; Jer. 1:5). Help us abide in this holy communion and extend it unreservedly to others.

Day 236

I maintain that all sorrow comes from love of those things of which loss deprives me.

MEDITATION

Possessiveness is the source of all our sorrow. Shorn of our sense of entitlement, God reveals His loving Presence to us in all things, even grief.

PRAYER

Help us to see all things, including life and death, as gifts from You, O God. You *'give and You take away'* with a wisdom and love beyond our understanding.

Day 237

Be ready at all times for the gifts of God, and always for new ones.

MEDITATION

Creation, like life itself, is a kaleidoscope of ever-changing, ever-fresh revelations of goodness and beauty. Only God can give us the eyes to see things this way (cf. Mt. 13:13; Jn. 9:25).

PRAYER

Grant us the gift of expectant faith, O God (cf. Heb. 11:1). Show us that our estimates of Your generosity are always woefully small.

A human being has so many skins inside, covering the depths of the heart. We know so many things, but we don't know ourselves! Why, thirty or forty skins or hides, as thick and hard as an ox's or bear's, cover the soul. Go into your own ground and learn to know yourself there.

MEDITATION

Our true selves are buried under countless layers of ego. We must discard these if we are to know our true selves in God.

PRAYER

Strip us of our egoic identifications so we can discover ourselves beyond the images we have of ourselves, O God. Help us to know ourselves as we are known by You (cf. 1 Cor. 13:12).

The ultimate and highest leave taking is leaving God for GOD, leaving your notion of God for an experience of THAT which transcends all notions.

MEDITATION

Words about God are not God, images of God are not God. Nothing is known of God apart from what He reveals. Even in His revelation, God remains Absolute Mystery.[35]

PRAYER

Help us discard our ideas of You to experience Your Presence, O God. Transcending our thoughts and words, You reveal Yourself in the stillness of our hearts.

---

[35] *'Absolute Mystery'* was Karl Rahner's favorite term to refer to the Mystery of God.

Day 240

This then is salvation - when we marvel at the beauty of created things and praise their beautiful Creator.

MEDITATION

God's Presence is glimpsed in the aliveness of things. God's grandeur is grasped in the beauty of creation.

PRAYER

Arrest us always with the grandeur and glory of Your creation, O God. In our awe at the sheer unexpectedness of things, we feel the touch of Your Presence.

Day 241

The soul will bring forth Person if God laughs into her and she laughs back to him. To speak in parable, the Father laughs into the Son and the Son laughs back to the Father. This laughter breeds liking and liking breeds joy, and joy begets love, and love begets Person, and Person begets the Holy Ghost.

MEDITATION

God is the Absolute Mystery of Being (*Sat*), Consciousness (*Chit*), and Bliss (*Ananda*). One with God, we abide in a state of *Satcitananda*.[36]

PRAYER

Grant us a share in *Satcitananda*, O God. Make us '*partakers of Your own divine nature*' (cf. 2 Pt. 1:4).

---

[36] *Satcitananda* (Sanskrit: सच्चिदानंद) is a Hindu expression meaning 'existence, consciousness, and bliss.'

Day 242

The Father and the Son have one Will, and that Will is the Holy Ghost, Who gives Himself to the soul so that the Divine Nature permeates the powers of the soul so that it can only do God-like works.

MEDITATION

God is diffusive of God's self. Our creation is a participative sharing in God's incomprehensible Life. We are sacramental extensions of God's ineffable Presence.

PRAYER

Help us recognize that every breath we take is an aspiration of Your Breath within us, O God. Help us see ourselves as in-breathed by Your divine Spirit.

Day 243

[The mystic/saint] is conscious only of God. To be conscious of knowing God is to know about God and self.

MEDITATION

We are as God is. Created in God's '*image and likeness*' (Gen. 1:26), we are finite icons of God's infinite Life.

PRAYER

We know You by participating in Your own self-knowledge, O God. Cultivating contemplative union with You, we know ourselves even as we are known (cf. 1 Cor. 13:12).

Day 244

If I had a friend and loved him because of the benefits which this brought me and because of getting my own way, then it would not be my friend that I loved but myself. I should love my friend on account of his own goodness and virtues and account of all that he is in himself. Only if I love my friend in this way do I love him properly.

MEDITATION

True love is bereft of any motivation other than being at the service of the beloved. Loving God, as well as loving others, is its own reward.

PRAYER

Purify our love of all possessiveness, O God. Divest us of every vestige of ego so we can love You and others with hearts void of self-seeking.

Day 245

There is no stopping place for anyone in this life, no matter how far along the way one has gone.

MEDITATION

The present moment is the only moment we ever have. It is never not Now. Every moment is a new beginning that never ceases being new.

PRAYER

Help us appreciate, and never fear, the unchanging freshness of the present moment, O God. *'When we've been there ten thousand years, it will be as if we've just begun.'*[37]

---

[37] From the song, *Amazing Grace.*

God is not good, or else he could do better.

MEDITATION

No human predicate applies univocally to God. God is good, loving, omniscient, and blissful, but in a way that infinitely transcends the way we experience them.

PRAYER

Comparisons with ourselves have no place in our contemplation of You, O God. Forgive us for imagining You after the fashion of our own image and likeness.

Day 247

We shall find God in everything alike and find God always alike in everything.

MEDITATION

It's a great thing to see God in everything, and even greater to see everything in God. This is the vision to which the Spirit beckons us.

PRAYER

Grant us a participative vision of reality, O God. Help us see all things as participating in Your Mystery of Divine Love that precedes and permeates creation.

I have sought earnestly and with great diligence that good and high virtue by which man may draw closest to God; and, as far as my intelligence would permit, I find that high virtue to be pure disinterest, that is, detachment from creatures. As Our Lord said to Martha, 'Unum est necessarium': one thing is necessary and that is disinterest.

MEDITATION

'Detachment' and 'disinterest' are stolid ways of describing the dynamic spiritual practice of maintaining childlike openness (*Gelassenheit*) to God.

PRAYER

Grant us a vibrant and vigilant openness to Your Spirit, O God. Empty our minds of our ideas of You so we can receive the fulness of Your revelation.

Day 249

If anyone went on for a thousand years asking of life, 'Why are you living?,' life, if it could answer, would say, 'I live so that I may live.' That is because life lives out of its own ground and springs from its own source, and so it lives without asking why it is itself living.

MEDITATION

God's is a why-less Love. God is who God is, and God does what God does. The only explanation for anything is a Divine Love beyond reason.

PRAYER

We stand astounded at the gratuity of being, O God. Why there should be something rather than nothing has no explanation other than Your why-less Love.

Day 250

And so, too, I speak of love: he who is held by it is held by the strongest of bonds, and yet the stress is pleasant. Moreover, he can sweetly bear all that happens to him. When one has found this bond, he looks for no other.

MEDITATION

Everything suffered for the sake of love is pure joy. It is love that transmutes raw pain into redemptive suffering.

PRAYER

Love redeems everything because You are love, O God (cf. 1 Jn. 4:8, 16). Help us recognize Your Presence in every movement of love in our hearts.

Day 251

My existence depends on the nearness and the presence of God.

MEDITATION

God is never finished creating us. Our existence is a continuous miracle of God's assent to our being.

PRAYER

We exist because You perpetually desire it so, O God. Reveal Yourself as the omni-present Source of our lives.

Day 252

One means of attraction which God uses is Emptiness, as we see when we place one end of a hollow pipe in water and draw up it by suction. The water runs up the stem to the mouth, because the emptiness of the pipe, from which the air has been drawn, draws the water to itself.

MEDITATION

Absence is always a form of Presence, revealing the truth of the one who is absent in a fuller way. Absence not only makes the heart grow fonder, but actually gives us the other in a way we could not otherwise know or appreciate.

PRAYER

Help us see that absence and emptiness are the unlikely space where You communicate deeper truth to us, O God. As with 'negative space' in art, it is out of the 'void' that beauty appears.

Day 253

What one takes in by contemplation, that one pours out in love.

MEDITATION

We cannot give what we do not have, and we have nothing we have not received. Contemplation is a gift of God's love and the source of everything we do in love.

PRAYER

Make our lives a continuous movement of contemplation-in-action, O God. Make us contemplatives who act, and actors who practice contemplation.

The love by which we love God is the very same love with which God has first loved us.

MEDITATION

'It is not that we love God, but that God has loved us first' (cf. 1 Jn. 4:10). Remembering the priority of God's love for us, not ours for God, is the foundation of the spiritual life.

PRAYER

Keep us from putting the 'cart' of our faith before the 'horse' of Your love, O God. Remind us that our trust in You is made possible by Your Love for us.

If you seek the kernel, then you must break the shell. Likewise, if you would know the reality of nature, you must destroy the appearance. The farther you go beyond the appearance, the nearer you will be to the essence.

MEDITATION

The Source of any object is both 'within' and 'beyond' the object. All contingent forms are sustained in their essential being by a Power greater than themselves. This 'Power' is what we call 'God.'

PRAYER

Direct our vision, not only beyond appearances but beyond all contingency, into the unconditioned mystery of Your Presence, O God. Show us that nothing exists that does so without You being transcendently present to it.

Day 256

All that God asks you most pressingly is to go out of yourself and let God be God in you.

MEDITATION

God is a Mystery of 'Allowing-ness' (*Gelassenheit*). All God asks of us is that we allow ourselves to be drawn into His infinite freedom.

PRAYER

Grant us *'the freedom of the children of God,'* O God (cf. Rom. 8:21). Inspire us to allow ourselves to be completely possessed by You.

Day 257

The person who has submitted his will and purposes entirely to God, carries God with him in all his works and in all circumstances.

MEDITATION

To 'submit' to God is to receive a share in God's infinite Abundance. We give ourselves to God so God can give Himself to us more completely.

PRAYER

Show us that in giving, we always receive more than we give, O God (cf. Lk. 6:38; 18:29-30). Remind us that You are a Wellspring of self-giving Love.

Day 258

Everything is full and pure at its source and precisely there, not outside.

MEDITATION

With God, 'above' is also 'within.' The transcendent Love of God is immanently present at the epicenter of every created form.

PRAYER

Awaken us to the paradox of Your transcendent and immanent Presence, O God. Show us that You are intimately one with us and infinitely beyond us at the same time (cf. Jn. 10:30; 14:28).

Day 259

Your own efforts 'did not bring it to pass,' only God. Yet, rejoice if God found a use for your efforts in His work.

MEDITATION

Like a mother asking her little daughter to help her bake a cake, God enjoins us to share in His creative work. There is nothing we do that is not done by God; yet, in all of this, it pleases God to have us as His co-creator.

PRAYER

Help us neither overestimate nor underestimate our human efforts, O God. Remind us that You are *'at work in us, both to will and to work for Your good pleasure'* (Phil. 2:13).

Day 260

Though [contemplation] may be called a nescience - an unknowing - yet there is in it more than all knowing and understanding without it. For this unknowing lures and attracts you from all understood things, and from yourself as well.

MEDITATION

True prayer means entering the *Cloud of Unknowing*, where God reveals a glimpse of His ineffable Presence.[38]

PRAYER

Show us how to pray in Your Spirit with a hunger and thirst *'too deep for words,'* O God (cf. Rom. 8:16). Take us beyond words and thoughts, images and ideas, and divinize us with Your uncreated Light.

---

[38] See above, n. 1.

Day 261

Love is as strong as death, as hard as Hell. Death separates the soul from the body, but love separates all things from the soul.

MEDITATION

'*Love is stronger than death*' (cf. Song 8:6). The essence of life is love, and the essence of love is dying to self (*Gelassenheit*).

PRAYER

Teach us how to die before we die, O God. Show us that life is only worth living when we have found that for which we are gladly willing to die.

Though one should live through all the time from Adam and all the time to come before the judgment day doing good works, yet he who, energizing in his highest, purest part, crosses from time to eternity, this man conceives and does far more than anyone who lives throughout all past and future time, because this now includes the whole of time. One master says that in crossing over time into the now each power of the soul will surpass itself.

MEDITATION

When we move from thinking to simple 'witnessing,' we experience the Presence and Peace of God. One moment of Presence is worth more than a lifetime of analysis.

PRAYER

Show us that all time in recapitulated and redeemed through the Power of the Now, O God.[39] Show us that time and space dissolve in the experience of Presence.

---

[39] See above, n. 3.

Day 263

Above thought is the intellect, which still seeks: it goes about looking, spies out here and there, picks up and drops. But above the intellect that seeks is another intellect which does not seek but stays in its pure, simple being, which is embraced in that light.

MEDITATION

Consciousness is infinitely more than thinking. When we become unbiased observers of our own thoughts, the kingdom of God dawns upon us.

PRAYER

Help us notice our self-transcendence, O God. Help us to know ourselves as infinitely more than the sum of our thoughts.

The man who dwells in one and the same light with God experiences neither suffering nor succession, but only an equal eternity. In truth, this man is bereft of all wonder and in him all things are present in their essence. Therefore he gets nothing new from things to come nor from any chance: he dwells in the single now which is all time and unceasingly new. Such a divine sovereignty is in this power.

MEDITATION

Mystical vision beholds the universe in a single grain of sand.[40] All time and space are present in the present moment for those *'with eyes to see'* (cf. Ezek. 12:2; Lk. 8:10).

PRAYER

Grant us mystical vision, O God. Help us to see You in the world, and the world in You.

---

[40] William Blake, *Auguries of Innocence*: '*To see a World in a Grain of Sand, And a Heaven in a Wild Flower, Hold Infinity in the palm of your hand, And Eternity in an hour…*'

Day 265

One must learn an inner solitude, wherever or with whomsoever he may be.

MEDITATION

External objects cannot give us inner purpose. Abiding in the depths of our being with God, the purpose of our lives is revealed, and the world becomes our footstool.

PRAYER

Reveal our personal vocations when we come before You with empty hands and willing hearts, O God. Deliver us from mindless chatter so we can hear the whispered wisdom of Your Spirit.

My children, mark me, I pray you: God loves my soul so much that His very life and being depend upon his loving me, whether He would or no. For God to stop loving me would rob him of His Godhood.

MEDITATION

God cannot *not* love. *'God is love, and those who abide in love, abide in God'* (1 Jn. 4:16). Since all people abide in God, God cannot be God without loving everyone infinitely.

PRAYER

Grant us the holy audacity - *parrhesia* - to trust unreservedly in Your irrevocable love, O God.[41] Show us You are more compulsive than ourselves when it comes to love.

---

[41] The term *parrhesia* (Greek: παρρησία *parrhēsía*) means *'to speak everything,'* *'to speak freely,'* *'to speak boldly'* or, simply, *'boldness.'*

It is a fair trade and an equal exchange: to the extent that you depart from things, thus far, no more and no less, God enters into you with all that is his. God enters into you only as far as you have stripped yourself of yourself in all things. It is here that you should begin, whatever the cost, for it is here that you will find true peace, and nowhere else.

MEDITATION

Self-emptying (*kenosis, Gelassenheit*) is where we make contact with God, since God Himself is an Absolute Mystery of *Kenosis* (cf. Phil. 2:7; Lk. 10:22). Divesting ourselves of self, we encounter the living, self-dis-possessing God.

PRAYER

Help us empty ourselves of our attachments that we may be filled with an abundance of Your Life (cf. Jn. 10:10), O God. Show us that in self-dis-possession we receive Your self-communication.

Day 268

I have often said that a person who wishes to begin a good life should be like one who draws a circle. Let him or her get the center in the right place and keep it so and the circumference will be good.

MEDITATION

Imagine God as the fine-tipped point of a compass. Our lives are the perfect circles He designs from the center of our being.

PRAYER

Anchor us in the epicenter of our hearts where You dwell within us, O God. Be both the center and circumference of our lives.

Day 269

Now the Father draws us from the evil of sin to the goodness of His grace with the might of His measureless power, and He needs all the resources of His strength in order to convert sinners, more than when He was about to make heaven and earth, which He made with His own power without help from any creature. But when He is about to convert a sinner, He always needs the sinner's help. 'He converts thee not without thy help,' as St. Augustine says.

MEDITATION

We must say Yes to God if our '*essential union*' with God at our creation is to become a '*transformative union*' with Him in our re-creation (cf. 2 Cor. 5:17).[42]

PRAYER

You created us without our assistance but will not transform us without our assent, O God. Grant us the grace to say with Mary, '*Let it be to me as You desire*' (cf. Lk. 1:38).

---

[42] See above, n. 15.

Day 270

Do not cling to the symbols but get to the inner truth!

MEDITATION

The rituals of religion are the outer shell in which the *'pearl of great price'* is contained (cf. Mt. 13:46). We must penetrate the facade of religion to enter the Mystery of Faith.

PRAYER

Keep us from becoming persons who *'hold the form of religion but deny the power of it,'* O God (2 Tim. 3:5). Draw us more deeply beyond the symbols of our religion into the Mystery which they convey.

Day 271

If anyone would ask me what God is, I should answer: God is love, and so altogether lovely that creatures all with one accord essay to love his loveliness, whether they do so knowingly or unbeknownst, in joy or sorrow.

MEDITATION

Created in the '*image and likeness of God,*' (Gen. 1:26), we incline to love by nature. '*God is love*' (1 Jn. 4:18, 16), and we are fulfilled by loving as God loves us (cf. Jn. 13:34).

PRAYER

'*In the evening of life we will be judged on love alone,*' O God.[43] Show us that all our human loves find their origin and end in You.

---

[43] Quote attributed to St. John of the Cross.

Day 272

If God gave the soul his whole creation she would not be filled thereby but only with himself.

MEDITATION

The gift is no substitute for communion with the Giver. God is greater than all the gifts He gives. The only gift that finally matters is union with God Himself.

PRAYER

Grant us the grace of transformative union with You, O God. Make us *'partakers of Your divinity'* in the same measure You have partaken of our humanity (cf. 2 Pt. 1:4).

Day 273

Where intuition finds, love follows, and memory and all the soul as well.

MEDITATION

It is with our hearts, not our heads, that we intuit the Presence of God. Ultimately, our love of God and our knowledge of God must coincide.

PRAYER

Grant us an intuitive apprehension of Your indwelling Presence, O God. Show us that 'within' is 'beyond,' and 'deep down' is 'above' when it comes to finding You.

Day 274

A pure heart is one that is unencumbered, unworried, uncommitted and which does not want its own way about anything but, rather, is submerged in the loving will of God.

MEDITATION

A certain, 'holy 'indifference' (*Gelassenheit*) characterizes the saints. Yet, this 'indifference' is not stoic resignation, but a childlike openness to God, uncluttered by anxiety or agenda.

PRAYER

Make us indifferent to anything other than being perfectly aligned with Your Presence, O God. Let nothing impede what You desire to do for, with, in and through us.

Love God, and do as you like, say the Free Spirits. Yes, but as long as you like anything contrary to God's will, you do not really love Him.

MEDITATION

Perfect union with God makes sin impossible (cf. 1 Jn. 3:9), yet perfect union with God cannot take place until we are emptied of our possessiveness.

PRAYER

You are at work in us *'both to will and to work for Your good pleasure'* (Phil. 2:13), O God. Strip us of the desire to possess anything other than what You desire for us.

The first means by which He draws is affinity, that affinity which brings creatures of the same species together and like to its like. With this cord of affinity He drew men to the Godhead, Whom He always resembles. In order that God may draw more to Himself, and forget His wrath.

MEDITATION

The greater our affinity with God, the greater our trust in His Love. *'God is love'* (1 Jn. 4:8) and *'perfect love drives out fear'* (1 Jn. 4:18).

PRAYER

There is no place for fear in our relationship with You, O God (cf. Lk. 8:25; Mk. 5:36). Strengthen our affinity with You so we can do nothing other than love.

Day 277

No man was ever lost except for one reason: having once left his ground he has let himself become too permanently settled abroad.

MEDITATION

When the branch is separated from the vine, it withers and dies (cf. Jn. 15:6). When the foundation is built on sand rather than rock it collapses (cf. Mt. 7:26-27). When our lives are grounded in anything but God, it is impossible for us to bear fruit as God desires (cf. Jn. 15:2, 8).

PRAYER

Keep us rooted in You, O God. Flourish us as You desire by keeping us connected to the Divine Vine of Your Presence.

Day 278

If the seal is pressed completely through the wax so that no wax remains without being impressed by the seal, then it becomes indistinguishably one with the seal. Similarly the soul becomes completely united with God.

MEDITATION

It pleases God to become so one with us that we can say '*it is no longer we who live but God who lives within us*' (cf. Gal. 2:20). God gives Himself to us according to our readiness to receive Him (cf. Jn. 14:23), while always remaining the separate Source of our deification.

PRAYER

As a clean window is translucent with the light, or a burning log incandescent in the fire, let us be divinized with Your indwelling Presence, O God.[44] Make us indistinguishable from You in our finitude with Your infinite Love.

---

[44] Images of the deified soul borrowed from the writings of St. John of the Cross. See especially, *Ascent of Mt. Carmel,* I, 10. 1-9; II, 14, 9; *Spiritual Canticle,* XXVI, 4, 17; *Living Flame of Love,* I, 3-4, 13, 19, 22-25, 33.

Day 279

The authorities teach that next to the first emanation, which is the Son coming out of the Father, the angels are most like God. And it may well be true, for the soul at its highest is formed like God, but an angel gives a closer idea of Him. That is all an angel is: an idea of God. For this reason the angel was sent to the soul, so that the soul might be re-formed by it, to be the divine idea by which it was first conceived.

MEDITATION

Our true identity is known only to God (cf. Eph. 1:12; Rev. 2:17). Our guardian angels are sent to keep us from identifying with anything other than the person God created us to be.

PRAYER

Make us attentive to the whisperings of Your Spirit, O God. Incline our inner ear to Your angelic summons to look to You alone for our true identity.

Day 280

By humility, out of an enemy He has made a friend, which is more than to have created a new earth.

MEDITATION

'*There is more rejoicing in heaven over one sinner who has a change of heart*' than over those whose hearts are already turned towards God (cf. Lk. 15:7). God takes special delight in saving us from our own undoing.

PRAYER

Awaken us to Your inescapable love, O God. Help us to see that there are no souls so far gone that You are not already there, saving them from themselves and carrying them home in Your divine Embrace (cf. Lk. 15:5).

Day 281

A just person is one who is conformed and transformed into justice.

MEDITATION

Actions speak louder than words. We must incarnate what we profess to believe if what we profess is to be believable.

PRAYER

In Christ, You became what we are so we could become what You are, O God. Make us images of the Image, icons of Your divine Love.

For then I knew my soul - every soul - has always held Him.

MEDITATION

One with God, we recognize every other person's intrinsic union with God. In God, we know everyone as our brothers and sisters.

PRAYER

Awaken us to our common paternity in You, O God. Help us experience Your Presence in every person we meet.

Let God operate in you. Hand the work over to Him and do not disquiet yourself as to whether or not He is working with nature or above nature, for His are both nature and grace.

MEDITATION

God does not distinguish between grace and nature, between sacred and secular. All is grace in God, all is holy in the eyes of God.

PRAYER

Let us despise nothing of what You have made, O God. Open our eyes to the beauty of everything we see, even that which has been disfigured by sin.

Day 284

Rejoice that you are so united with God that no one may separate you from Him. I cannot fully praise nor love Him, therefore must I die, and cast myself into the divine void, till I rise from non-existence to existence.

MEDITATION

Dying from love is the best way to go. Divine bliss bursts the hearts of those who experience it.

PRAYER

Life is not long enough for us to adequately sing Your praise, O God. Assume us into heaven so our praise of You can be made complete.

Knowledge comes through likeness. And so because the soul may know everything, it is never at rest until it comes to the original idea, in which all things are one. And there it comes to rest in God.

MEDITATION

In our quest for beauty, goodness and truth, we are constantly reaching beyond ourselves for something absolute. God is the Absolute for which we are searching.[45]

PRAYER

Awaken us to Your Presence in our self-transcendence, O God. Show us that it us You for whom we are searching when we grasp for things to satisfy our restlessness.

---

[45] See above, n. 26.

All that the Eternal Father teaches and reveals is His being, His nature, and His Godhead, which He manifests to us in His Son, and teaches us that we are also His Son.

MEDITATION

Our non-identical seamlessness with God is the great paradox of the spiritual life. Abiding in God, and God in us, we become fully who we are, even as God remains uniquely what He is.

PRAYER

Awaken us to our essential coinherence with You, O God. Help us to live in blissful, differentiated communion with You.

Day 287

Even stones have a love, a love that seeks the ground.

MEDITATION

Everything that has being emanates from consciousness, since creation emanates from God. Every creature knows and glorifies God according to its own form of awareness.

PRAYER

Show us that it is no mere metaphor to proclaim that *'all creation blesses You,'* O God (cf. Isa. 44:23; Ps. 148). Let our voices blend with the symphonic praise of creation.

Day 288

Words derive their power from the original word.

MEDITATION

God spoke and the entire cosmos came to be (cf. Gen. 1). Every being in the created world is a 'word' perfectly spoken by the Creator.

PRAYER

Show us how the world is in-breathed by Your Spirit, O God. Help us recognize Your voice in the whispering pines and flowers of the field.

Day 289

If we keep our eyes fixed on God alone, then truly he must work in us and nothing, neither the crowd nor any place can hinder him in this.

MEDITATION

Keeping our eyes fixed on God can be quite a challenge. Yet, the very desire to do so, even when not explicit, is God at work within us.

PRAYER

Your ways are inexplicable and inexorable, O God. Teach us to relax into Your prevenient Presence always at work in us for our salvation.

Day 290

Only he to whom God is present in everything and who employs his reason in the highest degree and has enjoyment in it knows anything of true peace and has a real kingdom of heaven.

MEDITATION

We discern God's Presence in everything, or we see the Presence of God nowhere. God's love is all inclusive - within and without everything that is.

PRAYER

Expand our awareness of Your ubiquitousness, O God. Reveal Yourself as present, not only in all things, but in our *presence* to all things.

Relation is the essence of everything that exists.

MEDITATION

Relationality is at the heart of who God is. God is always *Emmanuel,* God-with-us. And, '*if God is for us, who can stand against us?*' (cf. Rom. 8:31).

PRAYER

Show us that we are enfolded 'prepositionally' into You, O God. Show us that You are '*in*' us and '*for*' us and '*with*' us always and everywhere.

God is in all things, but so far as God is Divine and so far as He is rational, God is nowhere so properly as in the soul - in the innermost of the soul.

MEDITATION

All things participate in the Life coming from God, but only *we* are made in God's *'image and likeness'* (cf. Gen. 1:26). As such we enjoy a deeply *personal* relationship with God, intended for our ultimate deification.

PRAYER

Awaken us to Your Presence in our presence to other persons, O God. Show us that human love is a dim intimation of Your Love for us.

Day 293

I may err but I am not a heretic, for the first has to do with the mind and the second with the will!

MEDITATION

Our desire for God always exceeds our knowledge of God. Our desire is infinite, our understanding is limited.

PRAYER

Move us from head to heart, O God. Though we know You with our minds only *'as in a mirror darkly'* (cf. 1 Cor. 13:12), You reveal Yourself in our hearts with an infinite abundance of Your Presence.

If one's spirit were at all times united to God in the power of the now, a man could never grow old. Indeed, the now in which God made the first man, and the now in which the last man is to perish, and the now in which I am speaking are equal in God and are nothing but one sole and same now.

MEDITATION

God is 'pure Act,' an ontic Source of ecstasy, continuously creating *ex nihilo* (out of nothing) and *ad infinitum* (forever and ever). It is never not Now for God, nor for us.

PRAYER

Awaken us to the creative actuality of the present moment, O God. Reveal Yourself as the Creator and Redeemer of everyone and everything at all times and in all places.

To be right, a person must do one of two things: either he must learn to have God in his work and hold fast to him there, or he must give up his work altogether. Since, however, we cannot live without activities that are both human and various, we must learn to keep God I everything we do, and whatever the job or place, keep on with him, letting nothing stand in our way.

MEDITATION

Awareness of God and awareness of what we are doing are not two different actions. All awareness is a participation in God's self-communication.

PRAYER

Show us that our presence to anything or anyone is simultaneously a participation in Your own Presence to us, O God. Reveal Yourself as the Source of our power of awareness.

Day 296

Some people prefer solitude. They say their peace of mind depends on this. Others say they would be better off in church. If you do well, you do well wherever you are. If you fail, you fail wherever you are. Your surroundings don't matter.

MEDITATION

For those who know Presence, the world is their cathedral. What goes on in church is but a ritualization of what they experience everywhere - union with God in Presence.

PRAYER

Show us that peace of mind is not geographically or ritualistically determined, O God.

Grant us a continuous awareness of Your Presence wherever we go.

Day 297

God is with you everywhere - in the market place as well as in seclusion or in the church. If you look for nothing but God, nothing or no one can disturb you. God is not distracted by a multitude of things. Nor can we be.

MEDITATION

Becoming aware of God's Presence is like entering the eye of a hurricane. It is discovering a space of stillness and peace amidst surrounding chaos.

PRAYER

Lead us into Your Presence, O God. Show us that Your kingdom of peace is to be found within us when we cultivate attentive, inner stillness (cf. Lk. 17:21).

He who can make distinction in God without number or quantity, knows that the three persons of the Trinity are one God.

MEDITATION

Difference is a source of delight, not division, within the Trinitarian Life of God. The perpetual movement and infinite diversity of creation are the overflow of God's internal, unfathomable delight.

PRAYER

Awaken us to Your beauty in the variety of creation, O God. Show us that the differences we see are meant to unite, not divide us.

Day 299

One person who has mastered life is better than a thousand persons who have mastered only the contents of books, but no one can get anything out of life without God.

MEDITATION

Whether in books or in the world, God's self-communication is known as something more immediate, and more personal, than what we can grasp with our minds. Knowledge of God is more of the heart than of the head.

PRAYER

Awaken us to Your existential Presence, O God. Show us, as C. S. Lewis said, that the person seeking for You is like the mouse in search of the cat.[46]

---

[46] From his autobiography, *Surprised by Joy*.

Day 300

When God sends his angel to the soul it becomes the one who knows for sure.

MEDITATION

It is with angelic delight that we discover our personal vocation. Angels are God's messengers directing us to those things we cannot *not* do without compromising the person God created us to be.

PRAYER

Guide us into becoming the persons You desired us to be '*before the foundation of the world*,' O God (cf. Eph. 1:14; Jn. 17:24). Grant us incontrovertible certainty about our personal vocation in life.

Day 301

The less you feel and the more firmly you believe, the more praiseworthy is your faith and the more it will be esteemed and appreciated. For real faith is much more than a mere opinion of man. In it we have true knowledge.

MEDITATION

Faith seeks understanding, but no amount of understanding is the equal of childlike trust in God. Faith, to be pure, transcends our thoughts.

PRAYER

Lead us into the darkness of Your uncreated Light, O God. Blind our minds with Your radiance, warm our hearts with Your Presence.

'Virgin' designates a human being who is devoid of all foreign images, and who is as void as he was when he was not yet. I say besides for a man to be a virgin does not take away any of the works he has ever done; of all this he keeps himself virginal and free, without impediment to the supreme truth, just as Jesus was free and void and virginal in himself.

MEDITATION

It is the purity of heart with which we say and do things that constitutes a virginal heart. God desires only virginal hearts.

PRAYER

Restore us to spiritual virginity, O God. Dispossess us of our attachments so we have hearts made pure with Your uncreated Light.

Day 303

To walk on not wondering if am I right or doing something wrong.

MEDITATION

Second-guessing ourselves or God is not what God desires. Scrupulosity is the opposite of childlike trust in God.

PRAYER

It is not our sacrifices You desire, O God, but hearts free from fear, doubt, and insecurity (cf. Ps. 51:16-17; Mk. 5:36). Help us live with confidence in You, '*forgetting what lies behind and straining forward to what lies ahead*' (Phil. 3:13).

Day 304

When someone goes out of himself to find God or fetch God, he is wrong.

MEDITATION

We need look no further than our own hearts to discover the Presence of God. For *'the kingdom of God is within'* (cf. Lk. 17:21).

PRAYER

Awaken us to the immediacy of Your Presence, O God. Impress upon us that *'even before a word is on our tongues, You know it altogether'* (Ps. 139:4).

If I had a friend and loved him because of the benefits which this brought me and because of getting my own way, then it would not be my friend that I loved but myself. I should love my friend on account of his own goodness and virtues and account of all that he is in himself. Only if I love my friend in this way do I love him properly.

MEDITATION

God's love is completely *kenotic* (self-emptying). Created in the '*image and likeness*' of God (cf. Gen. 1:26), we glorify God most when we give of completely ourselves.

PRAYER

Show us that true friendship partakes of Your self-dis-possessing Love, O God. Help us love others as Your love, i.e., with divinely self-emptying love (*Gelassenheit*).

Day 306

The most powerful form of prayer, and the one which can virtually gain all things and which is the worthiest work of all, is that which flows from a free mind. The freer the mind is, the more powerful and worthy, the more useful, praiseworthy and perfect the prayer and the work become. A free mind can achieve all things.

MEDITATION

Thoughts becloud our vision, causing us to resist the form of the present moment. Hearts unimpeded by pesky mind-streams afford the clearest spiritual vision.

PRAYER

Dispel the clouds of our troubled minds with the brilliance of Your uncreated Light, O God. Give us spiritual vision unobscured with mental misgivings.

Day 307

Sensing God's presence is not in your power but in his. He will show himself when it suits him to do so, and he can also remain hidden if that is his wish. This is what Christ meant when he said to Nicodemus: 'The spirit breathes where it will: you hear its voice but do not know where it comes from, or where it is going' (Jn. 3:8).

MEDITATION

We discern God's Presence with sudden surprise when we relinquish our ideas and requests of God. God appears, not on demand, but when we cease desiring anything of God.

PRAYER

You are the Source and Summit of our hopes and dreams, O God. Continue to work in us both the impetus and the achievement of all Your desire for us (cf. Phil. 2:13).

Day 308

This real possession of God is to be found in the heart, in an inner motion of the spirit towards him and striving for him, and not just in thinking about him always and in the same way.

MEDITATION

Thinking about God gets us nowhere when uncoupled from contemplative prayer. Abiding with God in the depths of our being is the true source of right thinking about God.

PRAYER

Enlighten us from above and below, O God. Flood our souls with Your illumination so our thoughts reflect the hidden depths of Your love.

Day 309

We should not content ourselves with the God of thoughts for, when the thoughts come to an end, so too shall God. Rather, we should have a living God who is beyond the thoughts of all people and all creatures.

MEDITATION

The Presence of God cannot be experienced, save by transcending our thoughts of God. First comes our encounter with the *living* God, then understanding of God's ways flows from it.

PRAYER

Keep us alive to the difference between our existential encounter with You and our after-the-fact conceptualizations, O God. May we not confuse our ideas of You with our experience of Your immediate Presence.

Day 310

God is nameless for no one can either speak of him or know him. Therefore a pagan master says that what we can know or say of the First Cause reflects ourselves more than it does the First Cause, for this transcends all speech and all understanding. God is being beyond being: he is a nothingness beyond being.

MEDITATION

God has no being as we have being. As the *Source* of all that is, God must never be confused or described univocally with His effects. We *receive* our being from God, not God from us.

PRAYER

Only by affirming Your absolute transcendence can we appreciate Your immanent Presence, O God. You, who are above all condescend at every moment to be utterly gratuitous, not only to us, but to *'the birds of the air and flowers of the fields'* (cf. Mt 6:26-28). For this we praise and glorify You!

Day 311

St. Augustine says: 'The finest thing that we can say of God is to be silent concerning him from the wisdom of inner riches.' Be silent therefore, and do not chatter about God, for by chattering about him, you tell lies and commit a sin. If you wish to be perfect and without sin, then do not prattle about God. Also you should not wish to understand anything about God, for God is beyond all understanding.

MEDITATION

Silence and reverence go together. In the Presence of God, what can really be said that adds value to what is revealed?

PRAYER

All creation falls mute before You, O God. If we break out in song, it is only because our joy cannot be constrained.

Day 312

If I had a God that I could understand, I would not regard him as God.

MEDITATION

Any god that can be described is not the true God. The God we worship is not just another one of the gods.

PRAYER

Forgive our meager conceptions of You, O God. Have pity on us when we speak of You as if You could grasp You, for when we speak like that *'we do not know what we are saying'* (cf. Mk. 9:6; 10:38; Lk. 23:24).

Day 313

Of God you can never have a sufficiency. The more you have of God, the more you desire. If you could ever have enough of God, so that you were content with him, then God would not be God.

MEDITATION

God is both the Source and Satisfaction of our desire for God. The more God communicates Himself to us, the more He makes us yearn for Him.

PRAYER

Make us capable of receiving Your infinite self-communication, O God. Make it possible for us to be transfigured with Your divinizing Presence.

Truly, to have committed a sin is not sinful if we regret what we have done.

MEDITATION

The moment we awaken to our sins, they lose their power over us. Sin is synonymous with unconscious behavior (cf. Lk. 23:34). When we awaken from our spiritual somnambulance, salvation appears in the form of relief and freedom.

PRAYER

Show us that no sin can withstand the light of self-awareness that comes from Your Spirit, O God. Show us that You allow us to fall asleep in our sins only so You can awaken us with Your Mercy (cf. Rom. 11:32; Gal. 3:22).

Day 315

Indeed, if you are rightly placed in the will of God, then you should not wish that the sin into which you fell had not happened. Of course, this is not the case because sin was something against God but, precisely because it was something against God, you were bound by it to greater love, you were humbled and brought low. You should trust God that he would not have allowed it to happen unless he intended it to be for your profit.

MEDITATION

So-called evil is permitted by God only that God may be glorified when He delivers us from it (cf. Jn. 9:2-3). *'God has consigned all men to disobedience, that he may have mercy upon all'* (Rom. 11:32).

PRAYER

In Your infinite mercy, deliver us from all evil, O God. Show us that the demonstration of Your saving Love is the only reason evil is permitted its temporary reign.

Day 316

When we raise ourselves out of sin and turn away from it, then God in his faithfulness acts as if we had never fallen into sin at all and he does not punish us for our sins for a single moment, even if they are as great as the sum of all the sins that have ever been committed. God will not make us suffer on their account, but he can enjoy with us all the intimacy that he ever had with a creature.

MEDITATION

God has no interest in our sins other than as they prompt us to reach out for His mercy. God never asks, 'What went wrong?' but only 'How can I help you now?'.

PRAYER

Remind us that *'there is more joy in heaven over one sinner who asks for a change of heart than over ninety-nine righteous* persons who see no need to do so (Lk. 15:7), O God. Show us that Your infinite mercy retains no memory of our sins.

Day 317

If God finds that we are now ready, then he does not consider what we were before. God is a God of the present. He takes you and receives you as he finds you now, not as you have been, but as you are now.

MEDITATION

God exhibits a kind of divine Alzheimer's: He cannot remember our sins.

PRAYER

Grant us a share in Your merciful amnesia, O God. Keep us from cursing the darkness of our sins by drawing us into Your marvelous light (cf. 1 Pt. 2:9).

Day 318

God willingly tolerates the hurtfulness of sin and has often done so in the past, most frequently allowing it to come upon those whom he has chosen to raise up to greatness.

MEDITATION

The greatest sinners make the greatest saints. Why? Because God's *'ways are not our ways'* (cf. Isa. 55:8). God suffers us to stray only so He can demonstrate His saving grace (cf. Jn. 9:2; Rom. 5:20).

PRAYER

Awaken us to Your love for sinners, O God (cf. Lk. 5:31; 19:10). Keep us projecting our scrupulosity onto You.

Day 319

Was there ever anyone dearer to or more intimate with our Lord than the apostles? And yet not one of them escaped mortal sin. They all committed mortal sin. He showed this time and again in the Old and New Testament in those individuals who were to become the closest to him by far; and even today we rarely find that people achieve great things without first going astray. And thus our Lord intends to teach us of his great mercy, urging us to great and true humility and devotion. For, when repentance is renewed, then love too is renewed and grows strong.

MEDITATION

Our weakness is God's opportunity. When will we accept the mystery that God allows all to sin that He may have mercy on all (cf. Rom. 3:9, 23; 11:32; Gal. 3:22)?

PRAYER

No sin is mortal for those who turn to Your mercy, O God. Grant us a sure and certain hope for eternal life, anchored in Your faithfulness (cf. Rom. 3:3; Gal. 2:16).

Day 320

God, who is faithful, allows his friends to fall frequently into weakness only in order to remove from them any prop on which they might lean.

MEDITATION

Of the many tricks of Satan, perhaps the most subtle is his ability to make us proud of our spiritual progress. We can be puffed up even as we seek to be humble.

PRAYER

Grant us a kind of spiritual osteoporosis, O God. Allow us to break as often as necessary to make us totally reliant on You, our Divine Physician.

Day 321

For a loving person it would be a great joy to be able to achieve many great feats, whether keeping vigils, fasting, performing other ascetical practices or doing major, difficult and unusual works. For them this is a great joy, support and source of hope so that their works become a product and a support upon which they can lean. But it is precisely this which our Lord wishes to take from them so that he alone will be their help and support.

MEDITATION

At a certain point, our religious *formation* becomes an obstacle to our spiritual *transformation*. God is always dissolving what is good in order to give us what is better.

PRAYER

Grant us a willingness to let go of our achievements, O God. Show us that the essence of spiritual growth is to possess nothing but receptive openness (*Gelassenheit*) to You.

Day 322

In no way do our works serve to make God give us anything or do anything for us. Our Lord wishes his friends to be freed from such an attitude, and thus he removes their support from them so that they must henceforth find their support only in him.

MEDITATION

We must discard our transactional ways of approaching God if we are to be transformed by God's grace. Only when we surrender our bargaining chips can God give us the kingdom He has prepared for us.

PRAYER

Forgive our attempts to find favor with You, O God. Remind us that it is '*not we who have loved You, but You who have loved us first*' (cf. 1 Jn. 4:10, 19).

Day 323

For God has not linked our salvation with any particular kind of devotion. Any one devotional practice has things which others lack, but the effectiveness of all good practices comes from God alone and is denied to none of them, for one form of goodness cannot conflict with another. Therefore people should remember that if they see or hear of a good person who is following a way which is different from theirs, then they are wrong to think that such a person's efforts are all in vain. If someone else's way of devotion does not please them, then they are ignoring the goodness in it as well as that person's good intention. We should see the true feeling in people's devotional practices and should not scorn the particular way that anyone follows.

MEDITATION

God works differently with every person. God accommodates Himself to the readiness of the persons who seek Him.

PRAYER

Remind us that *'to compare is to despair,'* O God. Keep us from comparing our devotion to that of others. Inspire us instead to trust in Your inscrutable, salvific, will (cf. 2 Tim. 1:4).

Day 324

God does not give us anything in order that we should enjoy its possession and rest content with it, nor has he ever done so. All the gifts which he has ever granted us in heaven or on earth were made solely in order to be able to give us the one gift, which is himself.

MEDITATION

The only thing God has to give is God Himself. What we call 'grace' is simply God's self-communication.

PRAYER

You give us Yourself so we can be one with You, O God. Show us that the purpose of creation is that You should be *'all in all'* (cf. 1 Cor. 15:28).

All the works which God has ever performed in heaven or on earth served solely to perform the one work, that is to sanctify himself so that he can sanctify us.

MEDITATION

We are created to be the dwelling place of God (cf. Jn. 14:23). Our sanctification is God's glorification (cf. Jn. 17:22).

PRAYER

You have chosen us *'before the foundation of the world to be holy and unblemished in Your sight,'* O God. (cf. Eph. 1:14; Jn. 17:24). Make us worthy of Your divinizing Presence.

Day 326

We should learn to see God in all gifts and works, neither resting content with anything nor becoming attached to anything. For us there can be no attachment to a particular manner of behavior in this life, nor has this ever been right, however successful we may have been.

MEDITATION

The spoils of success pale in comparison to the bliss we receive when we surrender completely (*Gelassenheit*) to the faithfulness of God. Trust in God is its own, infinite reward.

PRAYER

Grant us a share in Your divine fidelity, O God. Help us to see that our trust in You is a participation in Your love for us.

Day 327

Some people are of the opinion that they are altogether holy and perfect, and go around the place with big deeds and big words, and yet they strive for and desire so many things, they wish to possess so much and are so concerned both with themselves and with this thing and that. They assert that they are seeking great piety and devotion, yet they cannot accept a single word of reproof without answering back. Be certain of this: they are far from God and are not in union with him.

MEDITATION

Defensiveness is a sure sign that we are not completely aligned with God. Those who know God know that nothing real can be threatened, and nothing unreal exists, therefore they are never defensive.

PRAYER

Free us from our defensiveness, O God. Immerse us more deeply in Your love so we realize that *'perfect love casts out all fear'* (cf. 1 Jn. 4:18).

Day 328

Truly, if someone were to renounce a kingdom or the whole world while still holding onto themselves, then they would have renounced nothing at all. Indeed, if someone renounces themselves, then whatever they might keep, whether the kingdom or honor or whatever it may be, they will still have renounced all things.

MEDITATION

Ego insinuates itself into all our activities, including our religious devotions. It is the renunciation of our possessiveness, not our possessions, that pleases God.

PRAYER

Grant us a share in Your divine *kenosis*, O God. Show us that when we relinquish our self-interest (*Gelassenheit*), Your Spirit possess us to '*the praise of Your glory*' (cf. Eph. 1:12, 14).

Day 329

Whoever does not truly have God within themselves but must constantly receive him in one external thing after another, seeking God in diverse ways, whether by particular works, people or places, such a person does not possess God. The obstruction lies within themselves, since in them God has not become all things.

MEDITATION

Breakthrough in the spiritual life occurs when we awaken to the fact that God is *'all in all'* (cf. 1 Cor. 15:28). All things were made through God, all things were made for God, and nothing - including sin - can separate us from the redemptive love of God made known in Christ Jesus (cf. Jn. 1:3; 1 Cor. 8:6; Rom. 8:38-39).

PRAYER

Direct us from our external pursuits of You to an interior discovery of Your Presence, O God. Help us to see You in the world, and the world in You, without confusion or identification.

Day 330

You should love God non-mentally, that is to say the soul should become non-mental and stripped of her mental images. As long as your soul is mental, she will possess images, and as long as she has images, she will possess intermediaries, and as long as she has intermediaries, she will not have unity or simplicity. If your inner being lacks simplicity, you do not truly love God, for true love depends upon utter simplicity.

MEDITATION

God is a Mystery of Absolute Love who desires us to love in simplicity of heart. *'Blessed are the pure of heart, for they shall see God'* (Mt. 5:8; Ps. 73:1).

PRAYER

Grant us a share in Your divine simplicity (*Gelassenheit*), O God. Help us love You with a purity of heart that transcends thinking and rests childlike in Your Divine Embrace.

Day 331

You must love God as he is One, pure, simple and transparent, far from all duality. We should eternally sink into this One, thus passing from something into nothing.

MEDITATION

The unity of God is the Source of the diversity we see in creation. Beholding all things as unified in God, we can let go of our fears and rest peacefully in God's Embrace (cf. 1 Jn. 4:18).

PRAYER

'Apart from You we can do nothing,' O God, but united to You *'all things are possible for us'* (cf. Jn. 15:5; Phil. 4:13). Deliver us from division and duality and draw us into harmonious unity with You.

Day 332

We should be able to recognize true and perfect love by whether or not someone has great hope and confidence in God, for there is nothing that testifies more clearly to perfect love than trust.

MEDITATION

Joy and confidence in God are the leading indicators of one's closeness to God. There is no such thing as a sad saint.

PRAYER

Deepen our intimacy with You, O God. Let our union with You overflow in hope, love, and joy.

Day 333

It is written: 'They have become rich in all virtues' (1 Cor. 1:5). Truly, this cannot happen unless they first become poor in all things. Whoever desires to be given everything, must first give everything away.

MEDITATION

In the economy of God, less is always more. Inner poverty and self-surrender (*Gelassenheit*) are synonymous with wealth in the eyes of God.

PRAYER

Enrich us with a share in Your own divine humility, O God. Show us that Your *kenosis* (self-emptying) is the instrument of our *theosis* (deification).

Day 334

You should not imagine that your reason can evolve to the extent of understanding God. Rather, if God is to shine divinely within you, your natural light cannot assist this process but must become a pure nothingness, going out of itself. Only then can God enter with his light, bringing back with him all that you have renounced and a thousand times more.

MEDITATION

It is when we let go of everything that we receive what God desires to give us. This is especially true of our understanding of God.

PRAYER

Darken our minds with Your uncreated Light, O God. Make us radiant with the splendor of Truth that transcends our ability to understand.

Day 335

If you understand anything about God, then he is not in it, and by understanding something of him, you fall into ignorance, and by falling into ignorance, you become like an animal since the animal part in creatures is that which is unknowing. If you do not wish to become like an animal, do not pretend that you understand anything of the ineffable God.

MEDITATION

Relinquishing our supposed knowledge of God, we are made ready to receive God's self-communication. We experience God's Presence when we stop pretending we know anything about God.

PRAYER

Show us that our knowledge of You is Your self-gift to us, O God. Make us grateful recipients of Your divine revelation.

Day 336

Undetached people say: 'It never works for me unless I am in this or that particular place and do this or that particular thing. I must go to somewhere remote or live in a hermitage or a monastery.' The lack of peace that such persons feel can only come from their own self-will, whether they are aware of this or not.

MEDITATION

Finding interior peace is not a matter of finding the perfect prayer space . Wherever we go, there we are, together with all our fears, doubts, and insecurities. Only interior surrender (*Gelassenheit*), not exterior travel, can bring us peace.

PRAYER

Grant us the grace of self-transcendence, O God. Show us that You abide with us, and we abide in You, wherever we happen to be (cf. Jn. 15:4-7).

Those who seek peace in external things, whether in places or devotional practices, people or works, in withdrawal from the world or poverty or self-abasement: however great these things may be or whatever their character, they are still nothing at all and cannot be the source of peace.

MEDITATION

Transformative union with God cannot be had through devotional practices alone. Such practices can sometimes be an obstacle to such union, since it is our interior detachment (*Gelassenheit*), not our exterior actions, that touches the heart of God and bring us His peace.

PRAYER

Keep us from idolizing our pious practices, O God. Show us that our divinizing union with You takes place when we surrender everything to You, including our religious devotions.

Day 338

If you hold to God, then he will give you goodness. If you seek God, then you will find both God and all goodness. Indeed, if you trod on a stone while in this state of mind, it would be a more godly act than if you were to receive the body of our Lord while being concerned only for yourself and having a less detached attitude of mind.

MEDITATION

Every action is sacramental for those who live in the world fully surrendered to God. Conversely, those who practice religion without an inner disposition of receptivity profane the Mystery and bring judgment upon themselves (cf. 1 Cor. 11:27–29).

PRAYER

Awaken us to the interiority of the spiritual life, O God. Help us handle all things in a sacramental manner that brings us closer to You.

Day 339

Whoever holds to God, holds to both God and all virtue. What was previously the object of your seeking, now seeks you; what you hunted, now hunts you, what you fled, now flees you. This is so because the things of God cling to those people who cling to God, and all those things flee them, which are unlike God and are alien to him.

MEDITATION

Virtue is a function of our closeness to God. No one can achieve union with God by trying to be good. On the contrary, all goodness we receive comes from our union with God.

PRAYER

'*You alone are good,*' O God (cf. Mk. 10:18). Help us to see that any good we do, or any desire to do good, comes from You (cf. Phil. 2:13).

Day 340

The more we are our own possession, the less we are God's possession.

MEDITATION

We do not belong to ourselves. All we have is gift, including our existence. We belong to God and exists solely for *'the praise of His glory'* (cf. Eph. 1:12, 14).

PRAYER

Show us that we are not the Source of our own existence, O God. Awaken us to the utter uncanny givenness of everything we have received.

Day 341

When we go out of ourselves through obedience and strip ourselves of what is ours, then God must enter into us. For when someone wills nothing for themselves, then God must will on their behalf just as he does for himself. In all things in which I do not will for myself, God wills on my behalf.

MEDITATION

The Greyhound bus company's motto is: *'Leave the driving to us.'* God says something similar: *'Leave the driving to Me.'*

PRAYER

Help us surrender control of our lives to You, O God. Bless us with the interior relinquishment (*Gelassenheit*) needed for You to direct us in all things.

Day 342

If we enter a state of pure nothingness, is it not better that we should do something in order to drive away the darkness and dereliction? Should we not pray or read or listen to a sermon or do something else that is virtuous in order to help ourselves? No, certainly not! The very best thing you can do is to remain still for as long as possible.

MEDITATION

In stillness, God speaks. Leaning to be present, learning how to listen, is the essence of the spiritual life.

PRAYER

Show us that *being* always precedes *doing*, O God. Show us that one minute of contemplative silence is worth more than a lifetime of frenetic action.

Day 343

Those who are in the right frame of mind, and for whom God has become their own, God will truly shine out just as clearly from their worldly acts as he does from their most sacred ones.

MEDITATION

The saint manifests holiness simply by walking around. Every gesture emanating from a divinized heart has the glory of God shining through it.

PRAYER

Saturate us completely with Your Presence, O God, so those who see us also see You (cf. Mt. 10:40; Lk. 10:16). Make our words and actions resplendent with Your goodness.

Day 344

However devoted you are to God, you may be sure that he is immeasurably more devoted to you and has incomparably more faith in you. For God is faithfulness itself – of this we can be certain as those who love him are certain.

MEDITATION

'It is not that we have loved God, but that God has first loved us' (cf. 1 Jn. 4:19). It is impossible to overstate the priority of God's love in our lives.

PRAYER

Deliver us from fashioning You into our own image and likeness, O God. 'If we who are evil know how to do good things,' how much more do You do good things for us (cf. Lk. 11:13)?

Day 345

They speak most beautifully of God who can maintain the deepest silence concerning him in the fullness of their inner wealth.

MEDITATION

The deeper our contemplative prayer, the more beautiful our actions. *'Out of the abundance of the heart'* the mouth of the saint speaks (cf. Lk. 6:45).

PRAYER

Draw us into the stillness of contemplative prayer, O God. Show us how to pray such that our actions glisten with Your divine glory.

God has not linked our salvation with any particular kind of devotion. Not everyone can follow the same way, nor can all people follow only one way, nor can we follow all the different ways or everyone else's way. It is the same with following the severe life-style of such saints. You can love the severe life-style of some saints and even find them appealing without having to follow their example.

MEDITATION

In the spiritual life, once size does not fit all. Our devotional profiles are as unique as our fingerprints.

PRAYER

Lead us to Yourself in the way best suited to the persons You have made us, O God. Grant us Your Spirit so we can discern the best path to You.

Day 347

It is hard counsel that we should not desire any reward. Be certain of this: God never ceases to give us everything. Even if he had sworn not to, he still could not help giving us things. It is far more important to him to give than it is for us to receive. God intends only that we should become yet more rich and be all the more capable of receiving things from him.

Meditation

In human relations it is generally '*better to give than to receive*' (cf. Acts 20:35), but in our life with God it is not so. God needs nothing of what we can give Him (cf. Ps. 50:10-13), but He has an irrepressible need to give us all that He has (cf. Lk. 15:31).

Prayer

Fill us with Your divine Life, O God. Show us that our vocation is to receive the glorification You have desired for us since '*before the foundation of the world*' (cf. Eph. 1:4; cf. Jn. 17:24).

Many people think that they are achieving great things in external works such as fasting, going barefoot and other such practices which are called penances. But true penance, and the best kind of penance consists in turning entirely away from all that is not God or of God in ourselves and in all creatures, and in turning fully and completely towards our beloved God in an unshakeable love so that our devotion and desire for him become great.

MEDITATION

A deep relationship with God cannot be developed with external works alone. Interior surrender (*Gelassenheit*) is the essence of true asceticism.

PRAYER

Grant us the humility of heart that touches Your heart, O God. Grant us a share in Your own self-dis-possessing Love.

Day 349

You should freely practice those kinds of works that help you raise your mind above all things into God. If any external work hampers you in this, whether it be fasting, keeping vigil, reading or whatever else, you should freely let it go without worrying that you might be neglecting your penance. God does not notice the nature of the works but only the love, the devotion and the spirit which is in them. God is not so much concerned with our works as with the spirit with which we perform them all and that we should love him in all things.

MEDITATION

God is interested in quality, not quantity. God sees the *desire* with which things are done for Him, not primarily *what* is done in His Name, since God has no need of anything we can do (cf. 1 Cor. 4:7).

PRAYER

Deliver us from our scrupulosity, O God. Grant us the freedom of spirit that allows us to love You and do what we will.[47]

---

[47] St. Augustine, *Sermon on Love.*

Day 350

They for whom God is not enough are greedy. The reward for all your works should be that they are known to God and that you seek God in them. Let this always be enough for you.

MEDITATION

God does not desire our works. God desires only that we desire Him with all our heart.

Prayer.

Show us that the essence of holiness is *holy desire*, O God. Show us that it is in the expanse of our yearning for You, not in our spiritual exercises, where You can be found.

Day 351

You should know that no one has ever renounced themselves so much in this life that there was nothing left of themselves to renounce. God enters into you with all that is his, as far as you have stripped yourself of yourself in all things.

MEDITATION

Self-emptying (*Gelassenheit*) has no bottom. Yet, God is one with us at the virginal point of our existence where, beneath all ego, we and God are one.

PRAYER

Strip us of self-interest, O God, so that we can know You as the Source and Sustainer of our true selves (cf. Col. 3:3). Destroy within us all that is not of You.

Day 352

We should keep all things only as if they had been merely lent and not given to us, without any sense of possessiveness, whether it be our body or soul, our senses, faculties, worldly goods or honor, friends, relations, house or home or anything whatsoever.

MEDITATION

It is our possessiveness, not our possessions, that impedes our divinizing union with God. Delivered from our covetousness by God's grace, we can enter freely into His rest (cf. Heb. 4:3-11).

PRAYER

We are *'anxious about many things'* other than our relationship with You, O God (cf. Lk. 10:41). Grant us an uncluttered love of You.

Day 353

If my eye is to discern color, it must itself be free from all color.

MEDITATION

'It is not that which the mind knows, but that by which the mind knows; not that which the eye sees, but that by which the eye sees; not that which the ear hears, but that by which the ear hears.'[48] Such is how we have knowledge of God.

PRAYER

Move us from object consciousness to space consciousness, O God. Teach us how to see all things in and through You.

---

[48] Paraphrase of the *Kena Upanishad.*

Day 354

In the very best kind of prayer that we can pray should be not 'give me this particular virtue or way of devotion' or 'yes, Lord, give me yourself or eternal life', but rather 'Lord, give me only what you will and do, Lord, only what you will and in the way that you will'. This kind of prayer is as far above the former as heaven is above earth. When we have prayed in this way, we have prayed well, having gone out of ourselves and entered God in true obedience.

MEDITATION

Docility to God's desires (*Gelassenheit*) is the goal of genuine prayer. We are on the path to sanctity when God's slightest wish becomes our dearest command.

PRAYER

Grant us a love that desires only what You desire, O God. Show us that the way to heaven *is* heaven for those who love You for Yourself alone.

Day 355

You should give your all to God, and then worry no more about what he may do with what is his.

Meditation

Giving everything away brings a share of divine bliss. God is the Absolute Mystery of self-surrender (cf. Phil. 2:6-11), and we are closest to God when we give ourselves completely to Him.

Prayer

'Take, Lord, receive all our memory, our understanding, our entire will. All that we are all that we possess, You have given us. We give it all to You to be used according to Your desire. Give us only Your love and grace and we shall be satisfied.'[49]

---

[49] Paraphrase of the *Suscipe Prayer* of St. Ignatius of Loyola.

Day 356

The more inadequate and guilty we perceive ourselves to be, the more reason we have to bind ourselves to God with an undivided love, who knows neither sin nor inadequacy. The greater we feel our sin to be, the more prepared God is to forgive our sin, to enter into the soul and drive sin away. Everyone is keenest to rid themselves of what is most hateful to them, and so the greater and graver our sins, the more God is immeasurably willing and quick to forgive them.

MEDITATION

It was because Divine Mercy always existed that it was necessary that those who would need mercy should be created, so that He who is Divine Mercy should not exist in vain.[50]

PRAYER

Your desire to forgive *precedes* our actual sins, O God. Is it too much to believe that You allow us to sin so that You may demonstrate the infinite depths of Your Divine Mercy (cf. Rom. 11:32; Gal. 3:22; Jn. 9:3)?

---

[50] Paraphrase of St. Irenaeus, St. Irenaeus, *Against the Heresies, 3.22.3.*

Day 357

When the repentance which comes from God rises up to him, all our sins vanish more quickly in the abyss of God than the eye can blink and are eradicated so totally that it is as if they had never existed.

MEDITATION

Sin, being an absence of good, has no substantial reality. It vanishes like the mist the moment our hearts turn towards God.

PRAYER

Grant us infinite confidence in Your inescapable love, O God.[51] Show us that the greatest sins cannot withstand the first flicker of repentance in our hearts.

---

[51] See Thomas Talbott, *The Inescapable Love of God*.

Day 358

Just as we can never love God too much, neither can we have too much trust in him. Nothing we may do can ever be so appropriate as fully trusting in God. He has never ceased to work great things through those who have great trust in him.

Meditation

Trust, not fear, must govern our every thought of God (cf. Mk. 5:36). Perfect trust drives out all fear (cf. 1 Jn. 4:18).

Prayer

Show us that fear of You offends Your infinite mercy, O God. Remind us that You are *'the Light in whom there is no darkness'* (cf. 1 Jn. 1:5), the *'Light the darkness cannot overcome'* (cf. Jn. 1:5).

Day 359

With God we can miss nothing. We can no more miss anything with God than God can. Accept the one way from God, then, and draw all that is good into it.

Meditation

Rooted in God we can do no wrong. Those completely surrendered to God '*do not commit sin, for God's seed abides in them, and they cannot sin because they are begotten of God*' (1 Jn. 3:9)

Prayer

Render us incapable of collusion with evil, O God. Unite us so completely with You that sinning against You becomes impossible.

Day 360

A perfect and true will can only exist when we have been entirely taken up into God's will and no longer have our own will. Whoever does this is truly rooted in God. Indeed, a single Ave Maria spoken in this spirit, when we have stripped ourselves of ourselves, is worth more than the repetition of a thousand psalters without it. In fact, a single step would be better with it than to cross the sea without it.

MEDITATION

Purity of heart is to will one thing.[52] Having no other wish than to do what God desires is the whole of the spiritual life.

PRAYER

Grant us the simple, childlike trust in You, O God. Let us desire nothing other than be led by Your Spirit.

---

[52] See Soren Kierkegaard, *Purity of Heart is to Will One Thing.*

Day 361

Those who cling to their own egos in their penances and external devotions, which such people regard as being of great importance. God have mercy on them, for they know little of divine truth! Such people are called holy because of what they are seen to do, but inside they are asses, for they do not know the real meaning of divine truth. They are esteemed by people who know no better. May they attain heaven because of their good intent, but that poverty, of which we now wish to speak, they know nothing.

MEDITATION

Poverty of spirit (*Gelassenheit*) is infinite wealth in the eyes of God. Only when we approach God with empty hands can God fill us with His transfiguring Life.[53]

PRAYER

Turn our attention from exterior devotions to our internal devotedness, O God. Show us that the thing You most desire is a '*humble and contrite heart*' (cf. Ps. 51:17; Mic. 6:8).

---

[53] See Henri Nouwen, *With Open Hands*.

God willingly endures all the harm and shame which all our sins have ever inflicted upon him, as he has already done for many years, in order that we should come to a deep knowledge of his love and in order that our love and our gratitude should increase and our zeal grow more intense.

MEDITATION

You permit sin so we may behold the unlimited scope of Your mercy, O God. No excuse for sin, this mystery is nevertheless breathtaking in its truth.

PRAYER

Awaken us to Your unfailing mercy, O God. Show us that the only sin against the Spirit is to believe than any sin - including that one - cannot be forgiven (cf. Lk. 12:10).

Day 363

You should know that God must pour himself into you and act upon you when he finds you prepared, just as the sun must pour itself forth, and cannot hold itself back, when the air is pure and clean. Certainly, it would be a major failing if God did not perform great works in you, pouring great goodness into you, in so far as he finds you empty and there.

MEDITATION

Our emptiness (*Gelassenheit*) attracts the fulness (*pleroma*, πλήρωμα) of God's Love. Nature may abhor a vacuum, but God does not. He rushes to fill those who turn to him who empty themselves of self-will.

PRAYER

Show us that we are created to be empty vessels for Your divine glory, O God. Fill us with the glory You have desired for us since '*before the foundation of the world*' (cf. Eph. 1:14; Jn. 17:22).

Day 364

You have to founder in your 'your-ness' to dissolve into God's 'his-ness.' Your proper self has to become so totally one Self with God's proper self that you understand God's being without any becoming, and His nothingness without any name.

MEDITATION

Our identity is *'hidden with Christ in God'* (cf. Col. 3:3). To live consciously with God, beneath and beyond the multiple layers of ego, is spiritual freedom.

PRAYER

Grant us a share in Your knowledge of Yourself, O God. Give us a glimpse of Your unconditioned Love.

Day 365

All creatures can very rightly say 'I,' for this is a universal word. But the word 'am' is different: no one can pronounce it properly except God alone.

MEDITATION

The being of creation derives from the primordial reality of God. Everything that exists participates in the self-subsistent Mystery of God who transcends, and yet is present to, everything that is.

PRAYER

Let us never cease to be astonished at the inexplicability of being, O God. Show Yourself to us as the ineffable Source, Order, and End of all reality - an infinite Wellspring of being, consciousness, and bliss.

Sources

Quotations used in this book, with their original references in the works of Meister Eckhart, can be found in the following sources:

AZ Quotes. Retrieved from: https://www.azquotes.com/author/4339-Meister_Eckhart.

Schürmann, Reiner. *Wandering Joy: Meister Eckhart's Mystical Philosophy*. Great Barrington, MA: Lindisfarne Books, 2001.

Sweeney, Jon M., Burrows, Mark S. *Meister Eckhart's Book of Secrets: Meditations on Letting Go and Finding True Freedom*. Charlottesville, VA: Hampton Roads Publishing, 2019.

_____. *Meister Eckhart's Book of the Heart: Meditations for the Restless Soul*. Charlottesville, VA: Hampton Roads Publishing, 2017.

Printed in the United States
by Baker & Taylor Publisher Services